Original title: 101 STRANGE BUT TRUE FOOTBALL FACTS

©101 STRANGE BUT TRUE FOOTBALL FACTS,
Carlos Martínez Cerdá y Víctor Martínez Cerdá, 2023

© Cover and illustrations: V&C Brothers
Proofreading: V&C Brothers

Writers: Víctor Martínez Cerdá and Carlos Martínez Cerdá (V&C Brothers)

Layout and design: V&C Brothers

All rights reserved. No part of this publication may be reproduced, stored in a retrieval system or transmitted in any form or by any means, mechanical, photochemical, electronic, magnetic, electro-optical, photocopying, information retrieval system, or otherwise, now or in the future, without the prior written permission of the copyright holders.

101 STRANGE BUT TRUE FOOTBALL FACTS

1

The history of soccer dates back more than 2,000 years in various ancient cultures, including Greece and Rome.

In Greece, a game called "Episkyros" or "Phaininda" was played, which involved two teams trying to move a ball made of goat bladder to the opposing field without using their hands.

The game was popular among young people and was played in sports festivals.

In Rome, the game of "Harpastum" was similar to Greek Episkyros and was played on a rectangular field with two teams and a small, hard ball.

The objective of the game was to carry the ball to the opposing field while preventing the opposing team from recovering it.

During the Middle Ages, different forms of soccer developed in England and other European countries.

One of the oldest games was "mob football," which was a violent and disorderly game played in the streets between residents of two neighboring towns.

In this game, players tried to move a ball towards a goal while the opposing team tried to prevent them from doing so.

2

In ancient times, balls were made from animal bladders or natural materials such as twigs or nutshells.

In the Middle Ages, players often used balls made of fabric filled with straw, wool, or even human hair.

Balls have also been made from sewn clothing filled with trash.

Nowadays, most balls are made from a combination of synthetic materials such as polyester, nylon, and rubber, and often contain an inflatable air bladder.

The modern design of a soccer ball consists of hexagonal and pentagonal panels sewn together to form a sphere.

As for where most balls are made, Pakistan has become a major center for soccer ball production in recent decades.

According to the Pakistan Sports Goods Federation, 80% of the world's soccer balls are produced in the city of Sialkot, in northern Pakistan.

There, hundreds of factories employ thousands of workers to manufacture soccer balls for world-renowned brands.

The boom in soccer ball production in Pakistan is partly due to cheap labor and the availability of low-cost materials.

However, the industry has been criticized for exploiting workers and for dangerous working conditions in some factories.

International organizations have worked to improve working conditions in the soccer ball industry in Pakistan and promote fair trade practices.

3

The Sheffield Football Club was the first registered football club in history and was founded in the city of Sheffield, in northern England, on October 24, 1857.

The club was founded by Nathaniel Creswick and William Prest, two former students of the Sheffield Grammar School.

Creswick and Prest had played football together while at school and wanted to create a club that could unite other young people in their passion for the sport.

The club's founding act, drafted by Creswick and Prest, established rules and regulations for the game, including the prohibition of touching the ball with hands and the need to score goals in a goalpost.

The club also established a set of principles and values for its members, including honesty and sportsmanship.

The Sheffield FC began playing matches against other local teams and quickly became a success.

The club also played an important role in the creation of the first rules of modern football, participating in the formation of the Football Association of England in 1863 and contributing to the development of the rules of the game.

The Sheffield FC still exists today and is considered a pioneer in the history of football.

The club has inspired many other teams and has left a lasting legacy in the world of football.

4

The Rungrado First of May Stadium is located in the city of Pyongyang, North Korea, and is considered the largest stadium in the world in terms of capacity.

It was built in 1989 and is primarily used for sports and cultural events.

The stadium has a capacity of 114,000 spectators and is designed in the shape of a lotus flower, an important symbol in North Korean culture.

The stadium's design also includes a retractable roof, which allows it to be used year-round, regardless of weather conditions.

Over the years, the stadium has hosted various sports events, including football and athletics matches, as well as concerts and cultural festivals.

One of the most notable events held at the stadium was the 1989 World Festival of Youth and Students, which featured the participation of more than 20,000 young people from around the world.

It is important to mention that the stadium is owned by the North Korean government and is primarily used for events related to the regime.

Additionally, it has been criticized for its construction and maintenance cost, which is estimated to be in the hundreds of millions of dollars, in a country where the majority of the population lives in precarious conditions.

5

Andoni Zubizarreta is considered one of the best goalkeepers in the history of Spanish football and is the Spanish player with the most appearances in the Spanish League.

Zubizarreta was born in Vitoria in 1961 and began his football career with his hometown team, Deportivo Alaves.

In 1986, he was signed by Athletic Club Bilbao, where he spent four seasons and won two Copa del Rey titles.

In 1990, Zubizarreta joined FC Barcelona, where he became the starting goalkeeper and helped the team win four Spanish Leagues, one UEFA Champions League, and several Copa del Rey titles.

During his time at Barcelona, he became the Spanish player with the most appearances in the Spanish League, with a total of 622 appearances over 17 seasons.

After his time at Barcelona, Zubizarreta played for other teams including Valencia CF and Deportivo La Coruna, before retiring from football in 1998.

In addition to his club career, Zubizarreta was a key player in the Spanish national football team, where he participated in three FIFA World Cups and two European Championships.

In total, he played 126 games for the Spanish national team.

Zubizarreta is widely considered one of the greatest Spanish goalkeepers of all time, and his record for most appearances in the Spanish League remains an impressive achievement.

6

Just Fontaine is a former French football player who is remembered for being the player who scored the most goals in a single edition of the FIFA World Cup.

He achieved this record during the 1958 World Cup in Sweden.

During that tournament, Fontaine played for the French national team and scored 13 goals in six matches, which remains an unmatched record in the history of the World Cup.

His goals were instrumental in helping France reach third place in the tournament.

During the group stage, Fontaine scored three goals in the match against Paraguay and two more in the match against Yugoslavia.

He then scored one goal in France's victory over Scotland in the quarter-finals, and two more in the semi-final against Northern Ireland.

In the third-place match, Fontaine scored four goals in France's 6-3 victory over Germany, making him the player who has scored the most goals in a single World Cup match.

Although Fontaine only played in one World Cup, his performance in Sweden 1958 made him a football legend.

His record of 13 goals in a single edition of the World Cup remains an impressive milestone in the history of the tournament.

7

**Recreativo de Huelva is the oldest football club in Spain,
and one of the oldest in the world.**

It was founded on December 23, 1889, by a group of young Englishmen who worked in the mines of Rio Tinto, a mining region in the province of Huelva.

The founding act of the club was signed at the old Hotel Colon in the city of Huelva, and since then, Recreativo has been an important part of the history of Spanish football.

The club has had its ups and downs throughout its history but has always been a source of pride for the city of Huelva and its fans.

The team has competed several times in the Spanish La Liga, and has had several notable players throughout its history, such as goalkeeper Jose Luis Chilavert and striker Kiko Narvaez.

It has also had some notable historic moments, such as its 3-0 victory over FC Barcelona in the 2006-2007 season.

The club is also known for its stadium, the Nuevo Colombino Stadium, which was inaugurated in 2001 and has a capacity of 21,670 spectators.

The stadium has hosted important matches of the Spanish La Liga and Segunda Division, as well as matches of the Spanish national team.

At the entrance of the town of Minas de Riotinto (Huelva), a sign welcomes travelers indicating: "Welcome to the birthplace of Spanish football."

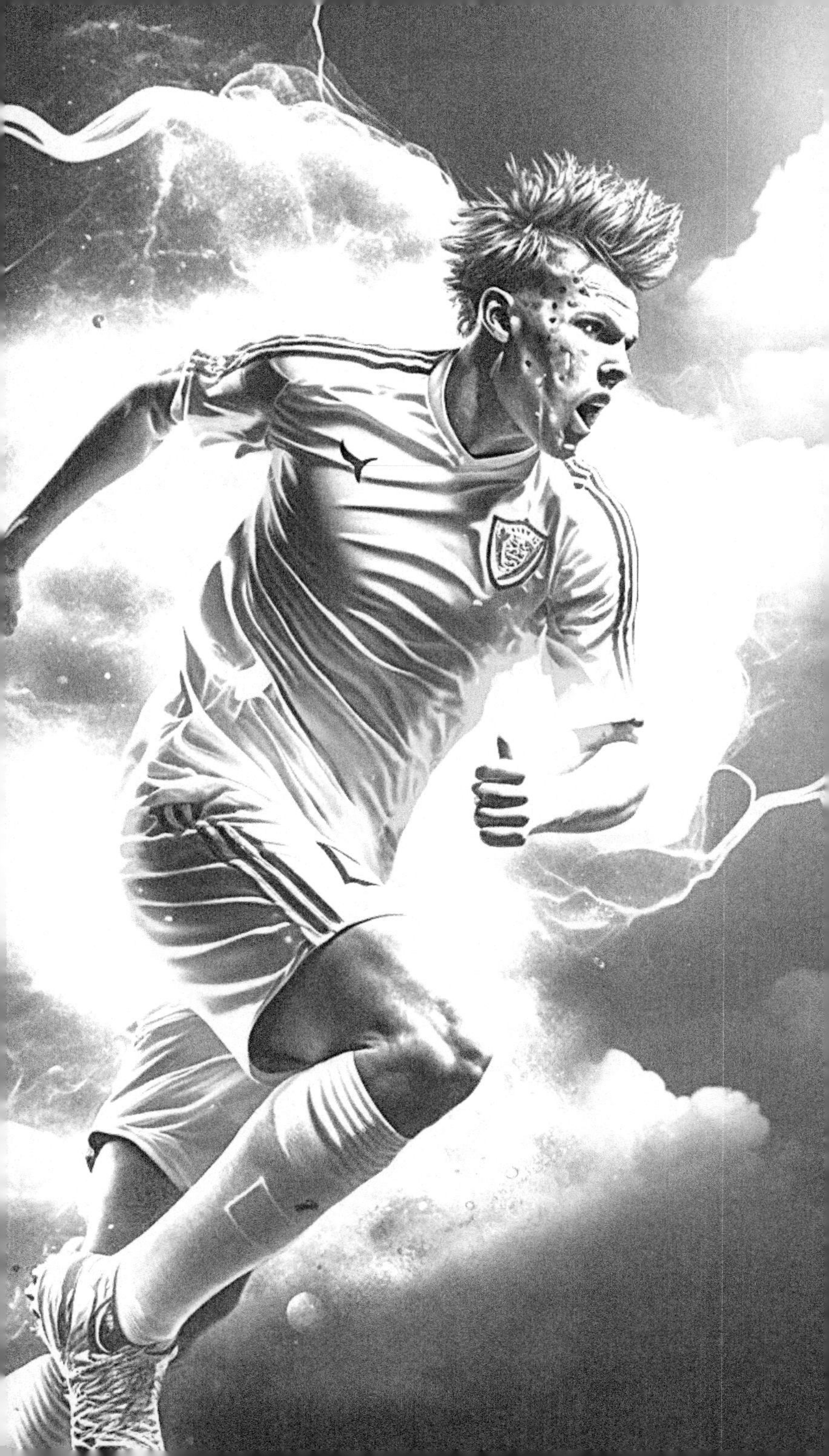

8

Neil Armstrong attempted to bring a soccer ball to the Moon.

It's said that Armstrong, who was the first human to step on the Moon during the Apollo 11 mission in 1969, had a great interest in soccer.

In fact, it's been said that he wanted to bring a soccer ball with him on the mission to play a sort of "lunar soccer game".

However, NASA did not allow Armstrong to bring the soccer ball to the Moon.

The main reason was the concern that the ball could damage the scientific and technological equipment that would be taken to the Moon, which could jeopardize the mission.

Additionally, NASA was also concerned about the weight of the ball, as any excess weight on the spacecraft could affect its ability to land and take off from the Moon.

Despite not being able to fulfill his desire to bring a soccer ball to the Moon, Armstrong's love for the sport has been well-documented.

In fact, it's said that in their free time during the Apollo 11 mission, Armstrong and his colleague Buzz Aldrin hit a golf ball on the Moon, which has been considered a historic and fun moment in the history of space exploration.

9

The fastest goal in the history of football was scored on December 26, 1998 in a match between the teams of Río Negro Capital and Soriano Interior, both from Uruguay.

The author of this historic goal was Ricardo Olivera, a player for Río Negro Capital, who scored after only 2.8 seconds from the start of the game.

This goal is recognized by FIFA as the fastest in the history of football.

The previous record belonged to the player Hakan Şükür, who scored in 11 seconds in the match between Turkey and South Korea in the 2002 World Cup.

Olivera's goal was made possible thanks to a quick and precise play by his team from the center of the field, where the ball was passed forward and Olivera received it with a chest control, followed by an accurate shot that went into the Soriano Interior's goal.

Despite the speed of the goal, the match ended with a 2-1 victory for Soriano Interior.

Olivera's goal will forever remain in the history of football as a memorable and exciting moment.

10

**Ahmed Hassan is a retired Egyptian footballer born
in the city of Maghagha in 1975.**

He is considered one of the greatest footballers in the history of Egypt and one of the most outstanding players in African football.

Ahmed Hassan began his career at the Egyptian club Aswan FC in 1993 and quickly became an important figure in the team.

In 1995, he was transferred to the club Ismaily SC, where he won several local titles and became the team's captain.

In 1998, Ahmed Hassan made the leap to European football and joined the Belgian club K.A.A. Gent, where he had a great performance and caught the attention of bigger clubs.

In 2000, he was transferred to RSC Anderlecht, where he won several league titles and became a key figure in the team.

In 2006, Ahmed Hassan returned to Egypt to play for Al-Ahly SC, one of the most successful teams in the country.

At Al-Ahly, Ahmed Hassan won several local and continental titles, including the CAF Champions League on three occasions.

Internationally, Ahmed Hassan is famous for having played the most matches for his national team, having played a total of 184 matches with the Egyptian jersey.

This record was held until it was surpassed by the Portuguese Cristiano Ronaldo in 2021.

Ahmed Hassan also participated in several editions of the Africa Cup of Nations with the Egyptian national team, being one of the standout players in the tournament.

In the 2006 edition, he was named the tournament's best player, helping his team win the title for the fifth time in its history.

After retiring from professional football in 2014, Ahmed Hassan became a football coach and has coached several clubs in Egypt and Saudi Arabia.

11

**The Football Association Challenge Cup, also known as the FA Cup,
is the oldest football competition in the world.**

The first edition of the FA Cup was held in the 1871-72 season and was
founded by C.W. Alcock, who was then the honorary secretary
of the Football Association (FA).

The idea behind the FA Cup was to create a national competition
in which all football clubs in England could participate.

The first edition of the competition featured the participation of 15 teams,
mainly from the London region.

The final of the first FA Cup was played on March 16, 1872,
and was contested by Wanderers FC and Royal Engineers AFC.

Wanderers won the final by a score of 1-0, becoming the first team
to win the FA Cup.

Since then, the FA Cup has become one of the most prestigious football
competitions in the world, and is seen as an important trophy
for both clubs and players.

The competition has seen many exciting moments throughout its history
and has been won by some of the biggest and most successful
clubs in England.

Currently, the FA Cup features the participation of over 700 teams, from
Premier League clubs to amateur and lower league teams.

The competition is played in a knockout format, with teams competing
in qualifying rounds and main rounds before reaching
the semi-finals and final.

The FA Cup final is held at the iconic Wembley Stadium in London
and is watched by millions of people around the world.

12

The farthest goal ever recorded in professional football was scored by Bosnian goalkeeper Asmir Begovic in a Premier League match on November 2, 2013.

Begovic scored the goal with an impressive shot from his own area towards the Stoke City goal, the team he played for at the time, and achieved a distance of 91.9 meters.

This goal is considered one of the most spectacular and surprising in the history of football.

Begovic's goal was scored just 13 seconds into the game, making it the fastest goal ever scored by a goalkeeper in football history.

The match was played against Southampton FC, and the goal was very important for the final result, as Stoke City won the match 1-0.

Begovic's goal generated a great deal of attention and admiration from football fans around the world.

The Bosnian goalkeeper became an instant celebrity, and his feat was recognized as one of the best and most exciting in the history of football.

Since then, other impressive long-distance goals have been scored in professional football, but Begovic's is still considered one of the most spectacular and surprising in the sport's history.

13

Pelé, whose real name is Edson Arantes do Nascimento, is considered by many to be one of the greatest footballers of all time.

Born in Brazil in 1940, Pelé began playing football from a young age and became famous for his exceptional skill and ability to score stunning goals.

Pelé was instrumental in establishing the so-called "Jogo Bonito" or "beautiful game," a style of football characterized by creativity, skill, improvisation, and elegance on the field.

This style of play became a hallmark of Brazilian football and is seen by many as a form of art.

Pelé played for the Brazilian national team for 18 years, between 1957 and 1971, and participated in four FIFA World Cups, in 1958, 1962, 1966, and 1970.

He won three of them, in 1958, 1962, and 1970, making him one of the most successful players in the history of the tournament.

During his career with the Brazilian national team, Pelé scored a total of 12 goals in the World Cup, a record that stood for many years.

He was also named the tournament's best player in 1970 and the best young player in 1958.

Pelé also had a very successful club career, playing for teams such as Santos in Brazil and the New York Cosmos in the United States.

During his career, he scored over 1,000 goals and won numerous titles and trophies.

14

A hat-trick is a term used in football to describe when a player scores three goals in a single match.

It is an impressive feat and is often seen as a display of the player's skill and quality.

Tommy Ross, a Scottish footballer, is remembered for his incredible achievement in a match played on November 28, 1964.

Ross scored a hat-trick in just 90 seconds, which remains a world record in football.

Ross played for the Ross County team in the Scottish Highland League, and the match in which he achieved this record was against the Nairn County team.

The match began with Ross scoring his first goal after just 20 seconds, followed by two more quick goals in the following minutes.

Although Ross never played in the Scottish League, his feat is still remembered and admired in the world of football.

Ross's record of scoring a hat-trick in 90 seconds remains unmatched to this day and is an example of the incredible skill and effectiveness of some players on the field.

15

The San Marino national team is one of the weakest football teams in the world.

San Marino is a small nation located in Italy, and its team has suffered a great deal of defeats in international competitions.

Since San Marino joined FIFA in 1990, they have played 109 official matches and lost 104 of them, only drawing five times.

San Marino has not won an official match since 2004, when they defeated Liechtenstein 1-0 in a friendly match.

Over the years, San Marino has lost many matches by big margins, including a 13-0 defeat to Germany in a Euro 2008 qualifying match.

The team has also suffered 10-0 defeats on several occasions, including a match against England in the 1994 World Cup qualifiers.

San Marino has had many coaches over the years, but none have been able to change the team's fortunes.

However, despite the adverse results, the San Marino national team has continued to fight in every match and has earned the respect and support of many football fans around the world.

16

The match with the most red cards in the history of football took place on December 14, 2013 in Argentina, in a regional league match between Claypole and Victoriano Arenas.

The referee of the match, Damián Rubino, issued a total of 36 red cards after a massive brawl broke out on the pitch after the match had ended.

The game had ended in a 2-2 draw, but tension had been building up throughout the game and erupted at the end.

Players from both teams started fighting and assaulting each other, which triggered a chain reaction of expulsions by the referee.

The previous record for the most players sent off in a professional football match was 19, and was set in the match between Sportivo Barracas and General Lamadrid in Argentina in 2011.

The match between Claypole and Victoriano Arenas and its record of 36 red cards has been widely covered by the media and has sparked a debate about violence in football.

Argentine football authorities have taken measures to try to prevent these kinds of situations in the future, including the introduction of stricter disciplinary measures and increased police presence at matches.

17

David Pratt is an English footballer who holds the record for the fastest red card in a football match.

The incident occurred on January 29, 2000, when Pratt was playing for Chippenham Town in a match against Bashley FC of the Southern Football League in England.

At the moment of the kick-off, Pratt committed a hard tackle on an opposing player and received a red card from the referee after only three seconds of the start of the match, making him the fastest player in history to receive a red card in football.

Pratt's tackle was considered dangerous and violent, leading the referee to make the decision to send him off immediately.

Pratt's action was heavily criticized and caused a stir in the media and in the football world in general.

Since then, Pratt's record has been difficult to beat, and his expulsion remains one of the most notable incidents in the history of football.

Pratt's action also serves as a reminder to football players of the importance of playing with fair play and respect towards other players on the field.

18

Oliver Kahn is one of the most famous and successful goalkeepers in the history of German football.

Born in Karlsruhe in 1969, Kahn began his professional football career at Karlsruher SC in 1987, before moving to Bayern Munich in 1994, where he would spend much of his career.

During his career, Kahn won numerous titles, including the Bundesliga, the German Cup, the UEFA Champions League, and the Intercontinental Cup.

But his greatest achievement came at the 2002 World Cup in Korea and Japan, where he led the German national team to the final, where they were defeated by Brazil.

Despite not winning the World Cup title, Kahn was awarded the tournament's Golden Ball, making him the only goalkeeper in football history to receive this prestigious award at a World Cup.

Kahn had an exceptional tournament in the German goal, conceding just one goal in the first six games of the tournament and making some crucial saves in the knockout phase.

The World Cup Golden Ball is awarded to the best player of the tournament, and it has typically been given to forwards or midfielders, as they are the players who usually score more goals or are more actively involved in the game.

Kahn's selection in 2002 was therefore especially significant, as it demonstrated the value and importance of a goalkeeper in a successful team.

Kahn retired from professional football in 2008, after a successful and outstanding career that makes him one of the greatest goalkeepers in the history of football.

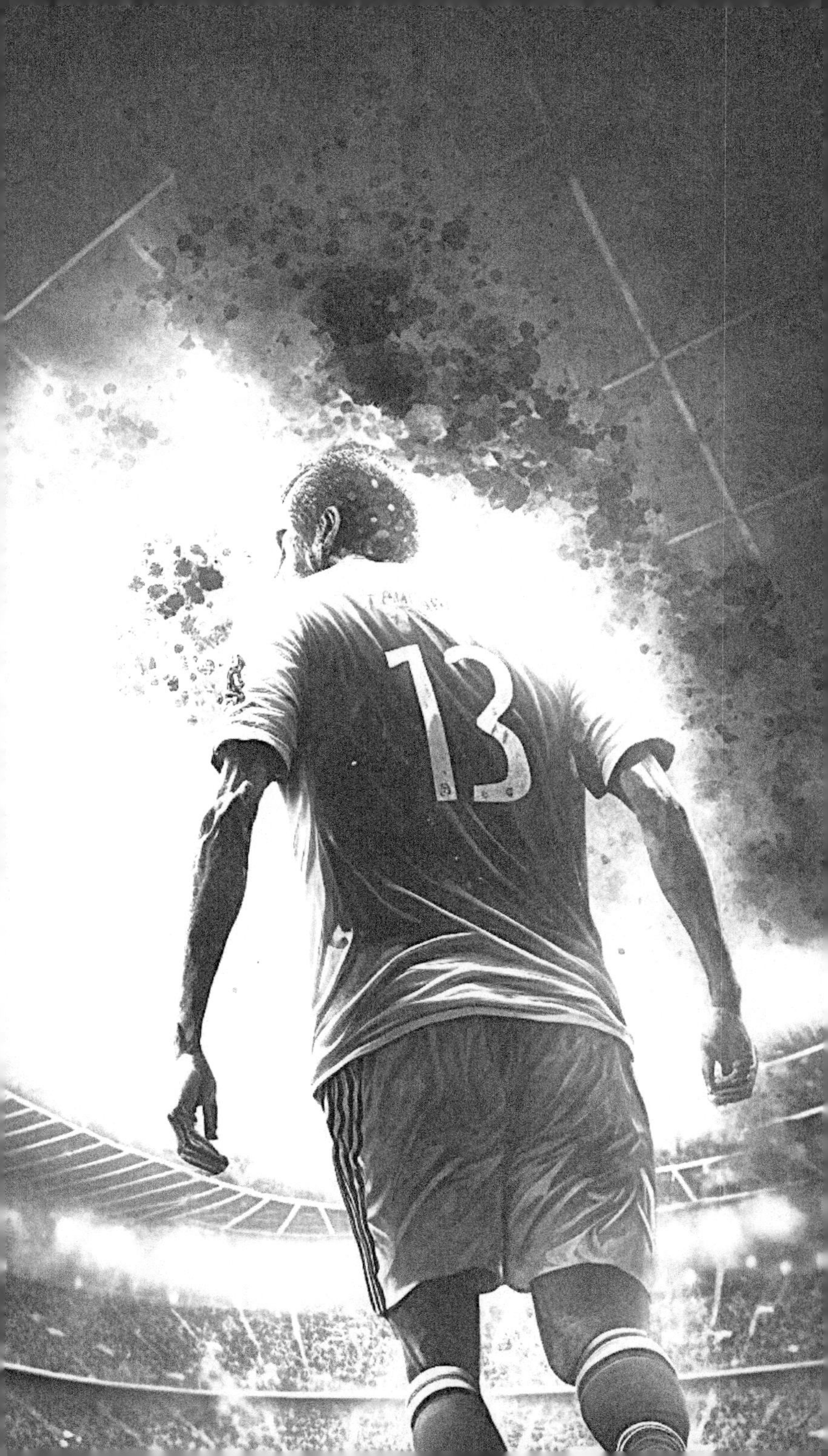
13

19

The Steaua Bucharest Football Club, also known as FCSB, is one of the most successful football teams in Romania, and its unbeaten streak is one of the most impressive in the history of the sport.

During that three-year period, Steaua Bucharest won three consecutive league titles, a European Cup, a European Super Cup, and a Romanian Cup.

In addition, during that period, the team not only did not lose any league matches but also did not concede more than one goal in any of them.

This streak began in August 1986 and ended in September 1989 when they finally lost to Dinamo Bucharest 2-1 in a league match.

During the 104 unbeaten league matches, the team scored 281 goals and conceded only 47, an impressive statistic that demonstrates their dominance at that time.

The coach who led this team during their streak was Emerich Jenei, and some of the standout players include Gheorghe Hagi, Marius Lacatus, Victor Piturca, Miodrag Belodedici, and Helmuth Duckadam.

20

On April 11, 2001, the Australian national team achieved the biggest victory in the history of international football teams in an official match.

They crushed their opponent, American Samoa, 31-0.

This sporting monologue was the largest win in an international match at that time.

The match was a qualifier for the 2002 FIFA World Cup and was played at the International Stadium in Sydney, Australia.

The Australian team dominated the match from the first minute and was already leading 16-0 at halftime.

Australian forward Archie Thompson set a record by scoring 13 goals in the match, making him the player with the most goals in an international match.

The result became a world record and remains the biggest victory in the history of international football teams in an official match.

Additionally, the American Samoa team had not trained together before the match and had very young and inexperienced players.

21

Neymar Jr.'s transfer to Paris Saint-Germain in 2017 was the most expensive in the history of football.

The signing was made for a record amount of 222 million euros, more than double the previous record, held by Paul Pogba's transfer from Juventus to Manchester United for 105 million euros.

Neymar Jr. became one of the highest-paid players in the world after his signing, with an annual salary of around 36 million euros.

However, his career at PSG has been marked by injuries and some off-field controversies.

22

The deadliest football disaster in history occurred at the Estadio Nacional in Lima, Peru, in 1964, during a match between the national teams of Peru and Argentina, which caused over 300 deaths.

Actually, the number of deaths varies according to sources, but it is estimated that at least 318 people were crushed or suffocated in the stampede that occurred when thousands of people tried to leave the stadium at the same time through a limited number of gates after the police launched tear gas to control a fight in the stands.

In addition, hundreds of people were injured in the incident.

This tragic event led to the improvement of safety regulations in football stadiums worldwide.

23

The tragic event happened on March 30, 1998, during a football match between the local team Bena Tshadi and the visiting team Basanga.

The stadium was located in a rural area of the Democratic Republic of Congo and was in poor condition.

During the match, it began to rain heavily and a lightning struck the pitch, instantly killing all 11 players of Bena Tshadi.

The players of Basanga, who were on the other side of the field, were unharmed.

This is considered one of the most tragic incidents in the history of football and left a great shock in the football community worldwide.

24

The first football match that was broadcast live on television was played on September 16, 1937, and it was a friendly match between the first team and the reserves of Arsenal at Highbury Stadium in London, England.

The BBC (British Broadcasting Corporation) broadcasted the match using two cameras and was watched by about 10,000 people who had televisions in their homes.

Since then, television has played a fundamental role in the dissemination and growth of football worldwide, and has allowed millions of fans to watch live matches from anywhere in the world.

25

The 2022 FIFA World Cup took place in Qatar.

The final of the World Cup was held in the city of Lusail, which is a city under construction on the outskirts of Doha, the capital of Qatar.

The stadium where the final was played is the Lusail Iconic Stadium, which is the largest stadium in the country and can accommodate up to 80,000 spectators.

26

Entel is a telecommunications company based in Chile that has been operating since 1964.

The company offers mobile phone services, internet services, and television services.

In 2018, Entel broke the Guinness World Record for the largest number of players in an exhibition match.

The event took place at the National Stadium of Chile and featured 2,357 players who kept the ball in constant motion for 120 hours.

The goal of the event was to promote physical activity and encourage a healthy lifestyle in Chilean society.

The exhibition match was a great success and attracted media attention from around the world.

The previous record for the largest number of players in an exhibition match had been set by a company in Japan in 2016, with 2,357 participants.

However, Entel surpassed this record by having the same number of players but keeping the ball in constant motion for 120 hours.

27

Washington Sebastián Abreu Gallo, commonly known as "El Loco" Abreu, is a Uruguayan footballer born on October 17, 1976 in Minas, Uruguay.

He plays as a forward and has played for multiple teams in various countries throughout his career.

Abreu began his football career in 1994 with the Uruguayan club Defensor Sporting.

Since then, he has played for many teams including San Lorenzo and River Plate in Argentina, Cruz Azul and América in Mexico, Botafogo and Figueirense in Brazil, Real Sociedad and Deportivo La Coruña in Spain, among others.

He has also played for various teams in his home country, such as Nacional and Danubio.

Abreu is known for his bold and creative playing style on the field, which has earned him the nickname "El Loco".

He is especially known for his skill in penalty kicks, having scored over 30 goals from the penalty spot in his career.

In addition to his club career, Abreu has also represented the Uruguayan national team on several occasions, including at the 2010 FIFA World Cup, where Uruguay reached the semifinals.

As for his record of playing for 31 clubs, it is an impressive achievement that is difficult to surpass.

Abreu has been a well-traveled player throughout his career, and has had success with many of the teams he has played for.

Although some may question his loyalty to a single team, it is undeniable that his career has been impressive and has left a mark on world football.

28

The Indian national football team is known for having withdrawn from participating in the 1950 FIFA World Cup, which was held in Brazil.

The official reason for the withdrawal was that they had not had enough time to prepare for the tournament, but it is rumored that the real reason was that FIFA did not allow Indian players to play barefoot.

Barefoot football was a common practice in India at that time, and many of the Indian team's players were used to playing without shoes.

However, according to the FIFA Laws of the Game, footwear is an essential part of a player's equipment and is considered a safety requirement to prevent injuries.

Although the true reason for India's withdrawal has never been officially confirmed, many believe that the footwear issue was the main factor.

At that time, the Indian national team was relatively unknown in the world of football and did not have a prominent history in the sport.

Additionally, the trip to Brazil would have been expensive and complicated for the players and the team.

Since then, India has not been able to qualify for the FIFA World Cup, although it has had some successes in other international football tournaments.

Football remains a popular sport in India, although it still faces challenges in developing and competing at the international level.

29

Charles Goodyear was an American inventor and chemist born in New Haven, Connecticut, on December 29, 1800.

At the age of 36, after many years of experimentation and trial and error, he discovered the process of vulcanization of rubber, which made it a much more durable and weather-resistant material.

The vulcanization process involves heating rubber with sulfur, which creates a chemical reaction that changes the molecular structure of the rubber and makes it more resistant and durable.

This discovery was a major breakthrough in the manufacture of a wide variety of objects, including tires, shoes, clothing, and condoms.

In 1855, Goodyear designed and built the first vulcanized rubber soccer ball, which was a major breakthrough in the sport's history.

Before this, soccer balls were made of leather and were very difficult to inflate and keep in shape.

The new vulcanized rubber ball was much more durable and resistant, making it ideal for use on the field.

The vulcanized rubber soccer ball became the industry standard in soccer and was used in the earliest international soccer tournaments and matches in Europe and North America.

Since then, technology has advanced, and other materials have been developed for the manufacture of soccer balls, but Goodyear's discovery remains an important milestone in the history of the sport.

30

Soccer is the most popular sport in the world and is played by a large number of people worldwide.

According to a FIFA survey in 2006, it was estimated that around 270 million people played football worldwide, and that number has been increasing since then.

Football is a sport played all over the world, and is especially popular in Europe, Latin America, and Africa.

It is the national sport in many countries, and is considered an important part of the culture and identity of many peoples.

In addition to being a very popular sport to play, football is also one of the most watched sports in the world.

Football matches attract a large number of spectators, both live and on television, and events such as the World Cup and the Champions League are followed by millions of people worldwide.

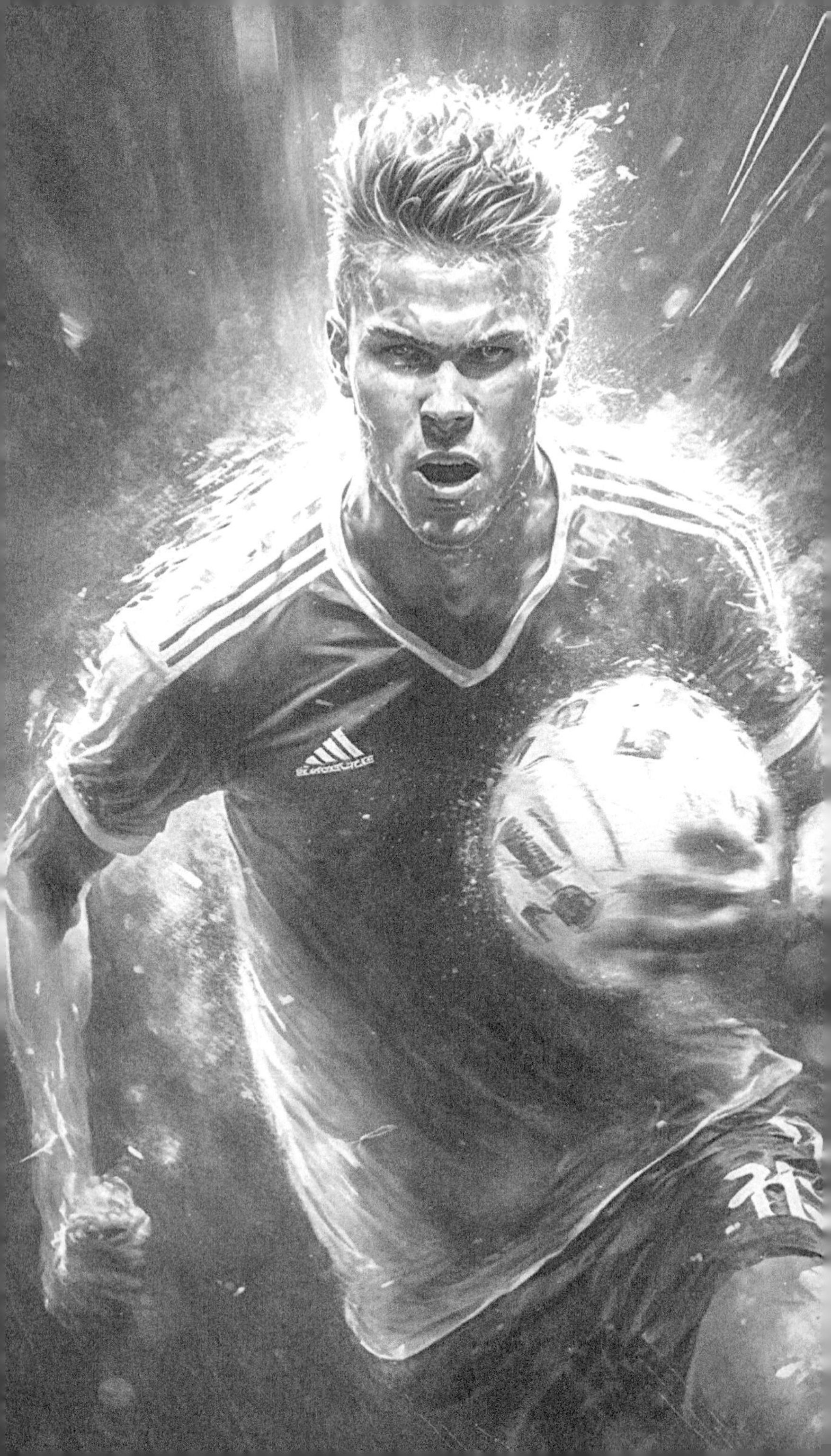

31

Some soccer players get injured while celebrating a goal, as there is often a lot of excitement and energy involved at that moment.

Celebrations can be very varied and sometimes include jumps, spins, runs, and quick movements, which can put the player's physical integrity at risk.

In fact, according to some studies, around 5% of soccer player injuries occur during goal celebrations.

These injuries can include ankle sprains, muscle strains, bone fractures, and head and spinal injuries.

To avoid injuries during celebrations, players often try to be more cautious and not overdo it with their movements.

It is also important for players to be in good physical shape and have good game technique to prevent injuries.

Despite the risks, goal celebrations are an important part of soccer and often become moments of great emotion for players and fans.

Players often have their own distinctive celebrations, and some of the most famous ones include Roger Milla's "frog jump," Peter Crouch's "robot dance," and Ronaldo's "heart celebration."

32

Eight of the 12 host cities where the 2014 FIFA World Cup took place in Brazil are among the 50 most violent cities in the world.

Brazil offered 25,000 hotel rooms to accommodate the demand from the 2014 World Cup and built 147 new lodging facilities in the host cities of the event.

According to a study by the Ministry of Tourism, 600,000 foreign tourists and three million Brazilians visited Brazil during the 30 days of the event.

33

Cristiano Ronaldo opened a museum dedicated to himself in his hometown of Funchal, on the island of Madeira, Portugal in 2013.

The museum, called CR7 Museum, is located near Funchal's port and has an area of around 400 square meters.

The museum displays numerous objects related to Ronaldo's football career, such as photos, jerseys, football boots, balls, and trophies, among others.

Some of the most important awards he has received throughout his career, like his three Ballon d'Ors, can also be seen.

In addition, the museum features a cinema room where a documentary about Ronaldo's life is shown, and an interactive area where visitors can play football and take photos with a wax figure of the player.

The idea of creating a museum dedicated to his career was Ronaldo's own, as he wanted a place where his most important achievements and memories could be displayed.

Since its opening, the museum has been a major tourist attraction on the island of Madeira and has received numerous visitors from around the world.

34

Preparing everything for the World Cup in Qatar has cost more lives than the terrorist attack on the Twin Towers, due to poor working conditions and inadequate infrastructure.

There have been reports of human rights violations and dangerous working conditions in the construction of stadiums and other infrastructure related to the 2022 FIFA World Cup in Qatar.

Deaths of migrant workers, mostly from Asian countries like India, Pakistan, and Bangladesh, who have been hired to build the facilities, have been reported.

There have also been concerns about lack of labor protection, exploitation and abuse of workers, as well as harsh working conditions in an extremely hot climate.

Measures have been taken to address these concerns, such as the implementation of a work permit system for migrant workers and the construction of housing for workers.

However, the situation remains under scrutiny and debate, and has led to increased attention to human rights in the construction of sports infrastructure and other major international events.

35

Former Brazilian forward Ronaldinho Gaúcho said the following when recounting a story from when he was 13 years old:

"I scored 23 goals in the same game, but the kids we played against were terrible. I think they only played in physical education class for fun and I was already on a team, which says a lot. It was in fifth grade and I have to say that it was never that easy again."

36

The first international football match between Scotland and England in 1872 is considered one of the most important moments in the history of football.

The match was played at Hamilton Crescent, Partick, Scotland, and was organized by the Scottish Football Association as a way to promote the sport.

The match was played under the rules of the English Football Association, as the official rules of football had not been standardized yet.

Each team had 11 players and the match lasted 90 minutes.

Despite the match ending in a goalless draw, it was considered a great success and helped establish football as a popular sport worldwide.

The game was watched by around 4,000 spectators, many of whom travelled from England to witness the event.

Since then, international football matches have become an important part of the sport, and have come to be regarded as some of the most important and widely followed sporting events worldwide.

National football teams regularly play friendly matches and FIFA tournaments, such as the World Cup, which is held every four years.

37

FIFA was founded in Paris on May 21, 1904, with the aim of organizing the world's most popular sport.

On that day, the founding document was signed by representatives from France, Belgium, Denmark, the Netherlands, Spain, Sweden, and Switzerland.

The function of FIFA is to draft and enforce the rules of football around the world, as well as to sanction the tournaments that take place.

Since 2016, the organization has rapidly evolved to become a body that can more effectively serve football for the benefit of the entire world.

38

In 2018, the newspaper El Mundo published an article claiming that FC Barcelona had paid seven million euros to the vice president of Spanish referees, Eugenio Enríquez Negreira, since 2001 for alleged verbal advice.

According to the newspaper's information, these payments were made through invoices issued by a company owned by Enríquez Negreira.

FC Barcelona strongly denied these accusations and stated that all payments made to Enríquez Negreira had been for legitimate and documented services.

In a statement, the club declared that "all of FC Barcelona's relationships with external suppliers have always been conducted within the law and in a framework of absolute transparency."

The Spanish Football League also commented on the matter, stating that it had no knowledge of any irregularities related to payments made by FC Barcelona to Enríquez Negreira.

However, these accusations generated a great deal of controversy and were investigated by Spanish authorities.

As far as is known, no evidence was found that FC Barcelona had acted illegally in relation to these payments.

It is important to note that refereeing in Spanish football has been controversial in the past, and some teams and fans have accused referees of favoring certain teams over others.

In this context, the accusations against FC Barcelona generated a great deal of media uproar and further fueled the controversy surrounding refereeing in Spanish football.

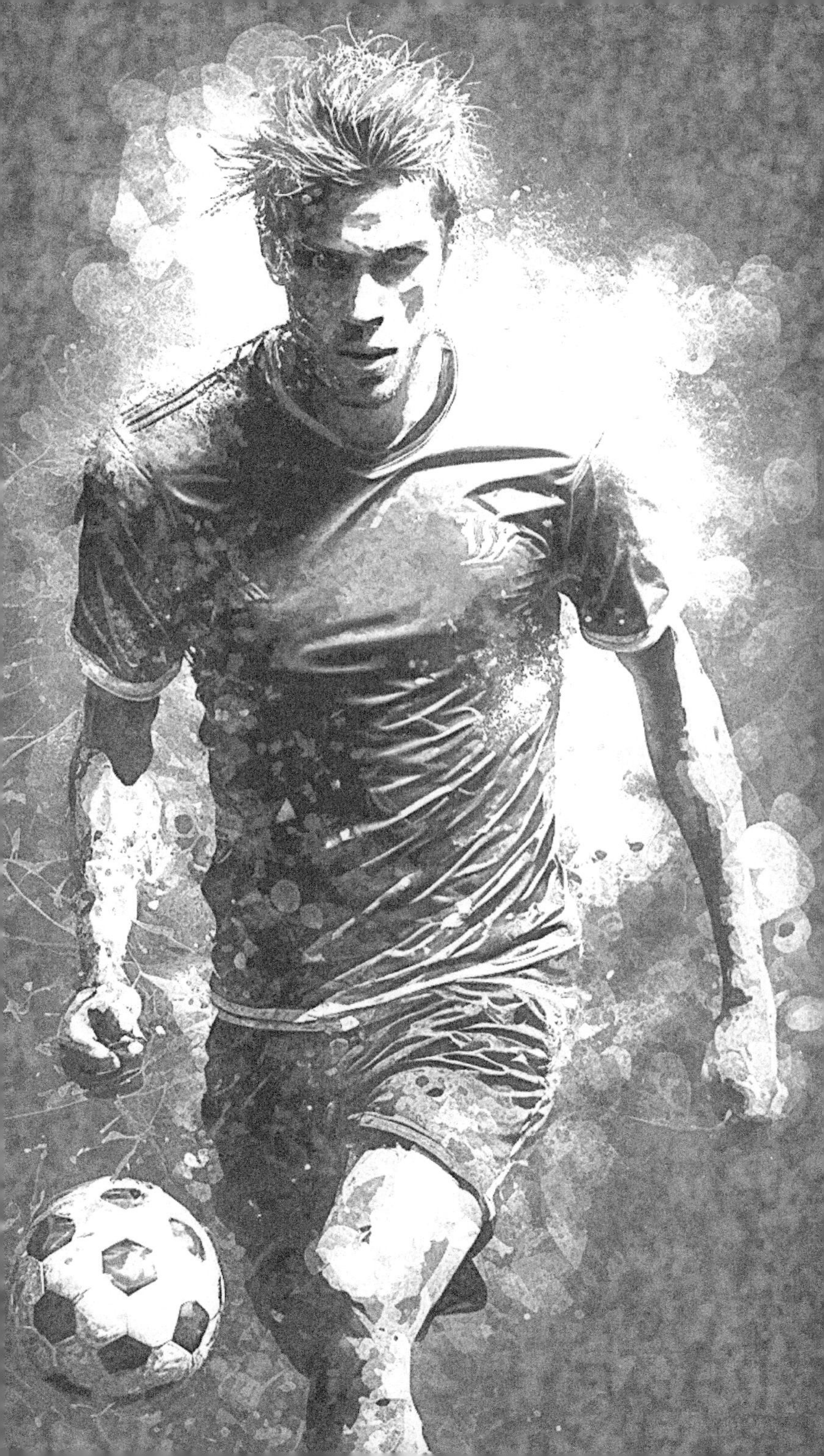

39

Franz Beckenbauer is considered one of the greatest footballers in history.

Born in 1945 in Germany, Beckenbauer excelled as a sweeper and playmaker, and is known for his technique, vision, and leadership on the field.

Beckenbauer played most of his career at Bayern Munich, where he won numerous titles, including three consecutive UEFA Champions League titles between 1974 and 1976.

He also won four Bundesliga titles and an Intercontinental Cup with Bayern.

In addition to his club success, Beckenbauer also had a successful international career with the West German national team.

He was part of the team that won the 1974 World Cup, where he served as captain and was instrumental in the team's defense.

He also played on the German teams that reached the final of the 1966 and 1970 World Cups.

After retiring as a player, Beckenbauer became a coach and continued to achieve success.

He led Bayern Munich to win the UEFA Champions League in 1996, and also coached the German national team that won the 1990 World Cup.

Beckenbauer has received numerous awards and accolades throughout his career, including the Ballon d'Or in 1972 and 1976, which is awarded to the best football player in Europe.

He has also been inducted into the World Football Hall of Fame and the German Sports Hall of Fame.

40

During his time, Pelé was the most famous and highest-paid athlete in the world.

He was an iconic figure who transcended the world of football and became a global ambassador for sport and Brazil. In the 1970s, it was estimated that Pelé earned over one million dollars per year in advertising contracts and sponsorships.

After retiring from football, Pelé continued to be an influential figure in sports and popular culture.

He has participated in numerous charity initiatives and has been an advocate for peace and equality around the world.

As for his fortune, Pelé is estimated to have a net worth of approximately $100 million.

Much of his wealth comes from his advertising contracts and sponsorships, as well as his career as a football player and coach.

Pelé has also ventured into other businesses, such as the music and fashion worlds.

In 2019, Pelé auctioned off much of his personal collection of football memorabilia and objects, including medals, trophies, and jerseys, which surely contributed to his fortune.

41

There is a floating football field in the small village of Koh Panyee, in Thailand.

The village is built on stilts over the water, and due to the lack of space on solid ground, the local inhabitants built a floating football field in the nearby bay.

The floating football field has become a popular tourist attraction in Thailand and has attracted the attention of several football teams from around the world.

One of the most famous teams in the area is Panyee FC, a youth team made up of local children who have excelled in national football tournaments.

The youth team of Panyee FC has won several regional and national championships in Thailand and has become a symbol of the determination and sporting spirit of the village of Koh Panyee.

The team's success has inspired other young people in the area to pursue their sporting dreams and has helped put the village on the map as a unique and exciting tourist destination.

42

Bolivian Mauricio Baldivieso was the youngest player to debut in the top division.

He made his debut in the Bolivian professional league in 2009 at the age of 12.

The lack of logic in the situation caused the club's management to prohibit the coach from fielding his son, which led to them leaving the club shortly after.

However, as their departure was a result of a heated decision, the player decided to return to the team, as did his father.

43

Stanley Matthews was a famous football player born in England in 1915 and died in 2000.

He is considered one of the greatest British footballers of all time and is remembered for his exceptional skill, speed, and technique.

Matthews began his career at Stoke City FC in 1932 and played for several clubs throughout his career, including Blackpool FC, Toronto City, and Stoke City again, where he retired.

He was also a standout player for the English national football team and played in three World Cups, in 1950, 1954, and 1958.

Despite retiring in 1965, Matthews returned to the field at the age of 50 to play one last game with Stoke City in 1965.

This makes him the oldest football player to have played a league game in England.

In addition to his success on the field, Matthews also received several honors and recognitions off the field.

He was the first British footballer to be knighted by Queen Elizabeth II in 1965, and in 2002, a stadium was inaugurated in his honor, the Stanley Matthews Stadium in Stoke-on-Trent.

In summary, Stanley Matthews was a legendary British footballer who left an indelible mark on the sport.

His longevity and dedication to football are an inspiration to many.

44

Kristof Van Hout is a Belgian footballer who currently plays as a goalkeeper for KVC Westerlo, a second division football club in Belgium.

Van Hout is known for being the tallest footballer on the planet, standing at a height of 2.08 meters.

Van Hout was born in the Belgian city of Lommel in 1987 and began his football career playing for his hometown local club.

In 2009, he was signed by Racing Genk, one of the most important clubs in Belgium, where he played for two seasons before being transferred to Standard Liege.

After playing for several Belgian clubs and a brief stint in the Indian football league, Van Hout joined KVC Westerlo in 2017.

Since then, he has become an important player for the club, thanks to his towering height and his skills as a goalkeeper.

In addition to his height, Van Hout is also known for his weight, which is around 110 kilograms, a common weight for people of his stature.

However, this has not prevented him from being successful in his football career and he has managed to play in different leagues and clubs.

45

Elton José Xavier Gomes, better known as Elton, is a Brazilian footballer who plays as an attacking midfielder.

He was born on September 5, 1986, in the city of São Paulo and became known in the world of football for his height, being considered the shortest player to have played in major South American and Asian leagues.

With a height of 1.54 meters, Elton has had to face unique challenges in his football career, as his low stature makes him more vulnerable in situations of physical contact with opponents.

However, this has not prevented him from being successful in his career.

He began his career in 2006 playing for the Brazilian second division club Fortaleza Esporte Clube.

He then went on to play for several clubs in Brazil, including São Caetano, América de Natal, and Mogi Mirim, where he stood out as one of the team's most skillful players despite his short stature.

In 2015, Elton moved to Asia to play for the Japanese club Vissel Kobe.

There, he became a key player for the team and helped lead the team to the final of the Emperor's Cup in 2017.

In 2018, Elton returned to Brazil to play for Bahia and then moved on to play for Red Bull Bragantino.

Despite his height, Elton is a technical and skillful player who has managed to stand out in the world of football for his talent and determination.

His career is a testament that size doesn't always matter in football and that perseverance and skill can lead to excellence in this sport.

46

Nawaf Al Abed is a Saudi footballer who plays as an attacking midfielder for the Al Hilal club in Saudi Arabia.

On October 21, 2017, Al Abed made history by scoring the fastest goal in professional football history.

The match was being played between Al Hilal and Al Shoalah for the Saudi League.

The referee blew the whistle to start the game and the opposing team made the first pass.

However, the ball was intercepted by Nawaf Al Abed, who shot on goal from the center of the field, surprising the opposing goalkeeper and scoring the goal just two seconds into the match.

This incredible goal by Al Abed broke the previous record for the fastest goal in football history, which was held by the Brazilian Fábio, who had scored in three seconds in a Brazilian league match in 2014.

Al Abed's achievement was widely celebrated in the world of football and became a historic milestone for Saudi football.

The goal showcased Al Abed's skill and vision on the field, who is known for his talent and ability to score goals from any position.

47

Greenland is the largest and northernmost region of Europe, located in the far north of the continent.

Despite its extreme climate, the Greenlandic population has a keen interest in football, and more than 10% of its inhabitants play this sport.

However, due to the region's climatic and geographical conditions, it has never been possible to cultivate grass on its football fields.

FIFA, the world football organization, requires football teams that want to be recognized by the organization to have appropriate playing fields, including high-quality natural or artificial turf.

Due to the impossibility of cultivating natural grass in Greenland, football teams in the region do not meet this requirement and therefore cannot be recognized by FIFA.

Despite this, football is very popular in Greenland and is played on gravel fields or in indoor sports courts.

Football is also one of the sports played in the Arctic Games, a sports competition held every two years and in which athletes from Arctic countries participate.

48

Referees were not used in official football matches until 1881.

Until then, the players themselves were responsible for performing that task.

They relied on the players themselves to arbitrate the game and ensure that it was played fairly.

This led to a great deal of controversy and fights, especially in the most important matches.

The first referee in an official football match was used in 1881 in a Football Association (FA) match in England.

The referee was an army officer named N.S. Lane, and his role was to make the final decisions on the field and ensure that the rules of the game were respected.

As football became more organized and popular worldwide, it became a common practice to have official referees in football matches.

These referees were responsible for making decisions and enforcing the rules of the game on the field, and were expected to keep the game fair and safe for all players.

49

The FIFA World Cup is the most important trophy in worldwide football.

It was designed in 1970 by the Italian sculptor Silvio Gazzaniga, and since then it has been the prize awarded to the winners of the most prestigious football tournament in the world.

The World Cup trophy weighs 6.142 kilograms and is made of solid 18-carat gold.

It has a height of 36.8 centimeters and a base diameter of 13 centimeters.

At the top of the trophy, two female figures can be seen holding up the Earth.

The manufacturing process of the World Cup trophy is very delicate and careful. The trophy is cast in solid gold and then shaped by hand.

The design is made with great precision and detail, and the manufacturing process can take several months.

The World Cup trophy is awarded to the winners every four years during the FIFA tournament.

The team that wins the tournament is entitled to keep the trophy until the next World Cup, where it is competed for again.

In the event that a team wins the tournament three times, they will be given a replica of the original trophy.

The World Cup trophy is a symbol of excellence and prestige in the world of football, and it is one of the most watched and followed sports events worldwide.

The tournament brings together the best football teams and players from around the globe and has become a global celebration of sport and fair competition.

50

Uruguay was the first country to win the FIFA World Cup in 1930, in a tournament held on their own soil.

At that time, only 13 teams participated in the tournament, and the Uruguayan team defeated Argentina in the final 4-2 to make history as the first world football champion.

However, four years later, Uruguay refused to participate in the 1934 World Cup, held in Italy.

The reason for this decision was the fact that Italy had not sent a team to participate in the 1930 World Cup in Uruguay, and the Uruguayan team felt it was a lack of respect from the Italians.

Because Uruguay refused to participate in the 1934 tournament, they did not have the opportunity to defend their title.

As a result, the Italian team won the 1934 World Cup, and Uruguay had to wait four years until the next tournament to try to regain their crown.

In the 1934 World Cup, only 16 teams participated, of which four were from non-European countries: Argentina, Brazil, the United States, and Egypt, which was the first African team to compete in the history of the World Cup.

51

Funny quotes from soccer players:

-**Carlos Tevez:** "As one wins things, you become a hamburger" (June 2017).

-**Edinson Cavani:** "Like any African team, Jamaica will be a difficult rival" (Copa America 2015).

-**Ronaldo Nazario:** "We lost because we didn't win".

-**Sergio Ramos:** "When we were kids, many friends liked basketball, and others liked basquetball".

-**Alessandro Altobelli (Italian striker from the 80s):** "Soccer is like chess, but without dice".

-**Nelson Pedetti (former Uruguayan player):** "I saw the goalkeeper advanced and I chipped it over him, it was a dentistry goal".

-**Murci Rojas (former Chilean defender):** "I can't say anything about the country I'm going to... I'll just say it's a Brazilian team".

-**Mostaza Merlo:** "How many lungs do I have? One, like everyone else".

-**Gustavo Biscayzacu (Uruguayan soccer player):** "Yes, I feel very good physically. That is, among other things, thanks to the diet provided by the nutritionist, based on hydrocarbons".

52

In the final match of the 1950 FIFA World Cup, in which Brazil and Uruguay faced each other at the Maracanã Stadium in Rio de Janeiro, at the time, the stadium was one of the largest in the world and had an official capacity of 150,000 spectators.

However, due to the high demand for tickets for the final, the organizers decided to temporarily expand the stadium's capacity, and it is estimated that around 200,000 people attended the match.

The match was a huge shock to Brazilians, as Uruguay won 2-1, depriving Brazil of winning their first World Cup on their own soil.

The result was considered one of the greatest upsets in football history, and the event is known as the "Maracanazo".

The attendance record of 200,000 spectators at the Maracanã Stadium in 1950 still stands as the highest number of people to have attended a football match to date.

Since then, the stadium's official capacity has been reduced to 78,838 spectators due to safety concerns, but it remains one of the most iconic stadiums in world football.

53

The Norwegian national team has an impressive record against Brazil in international competitions, with two wins and two draws in the four matches they have played to date.

The first match between Norway and Brazil was played in the group stage of the 1998 World Cup in France, and Norway surprised the football world by beating the Brazilian team, who would later reach the final of the tournament, 2-1.

The second encounter was a friendly played in 1997, in which Norway and Brazil drew 1-1.

The third time they faced each other was in a friendly in 2006, in which Norway won 2-1.

The last match between both teams was another 1-1 draw in a friendly in 2012.

It should be noted that despite this good streak against Brazil, Norway has never won a major title in world football, while Brazil is one of the most successful teams in the history of football, having won the World Cup on five occasions.

54

There are over 5,000 teams in the English football system with different levels, depending on the game category.

It is one of the largest and most complex in the world, and consists of several divisions and categories.

The Premier League is the highest professional football league in England, with 20 teams competing each season for the title.

Below the Premier League are the EFL Championship, EFL League One, and EFL League Two, which are the professional leagues of the second, third, and fourth divisions, respectively.

In addition to these leagues, there are several cup competitions in England, such as the FA Cup and EFL Cup, in which teams from different levels of the English football system participate.

There are also non-professional leagues in the English football system, which include amateur and semi-professional teams.

These leagues are organized by the English Football Association (FA) and are divided into various levels and regional divisions.

As for age categories, youth teams are usually made up of players between 16 and 18 years old, cadets between 14 and 15 years old, juniors between 12 and 13 years old, and minors between 10 and 11 years old.

Each category has its own competitions and tournaments, and players can progress through the different categories based on their age and football skills.

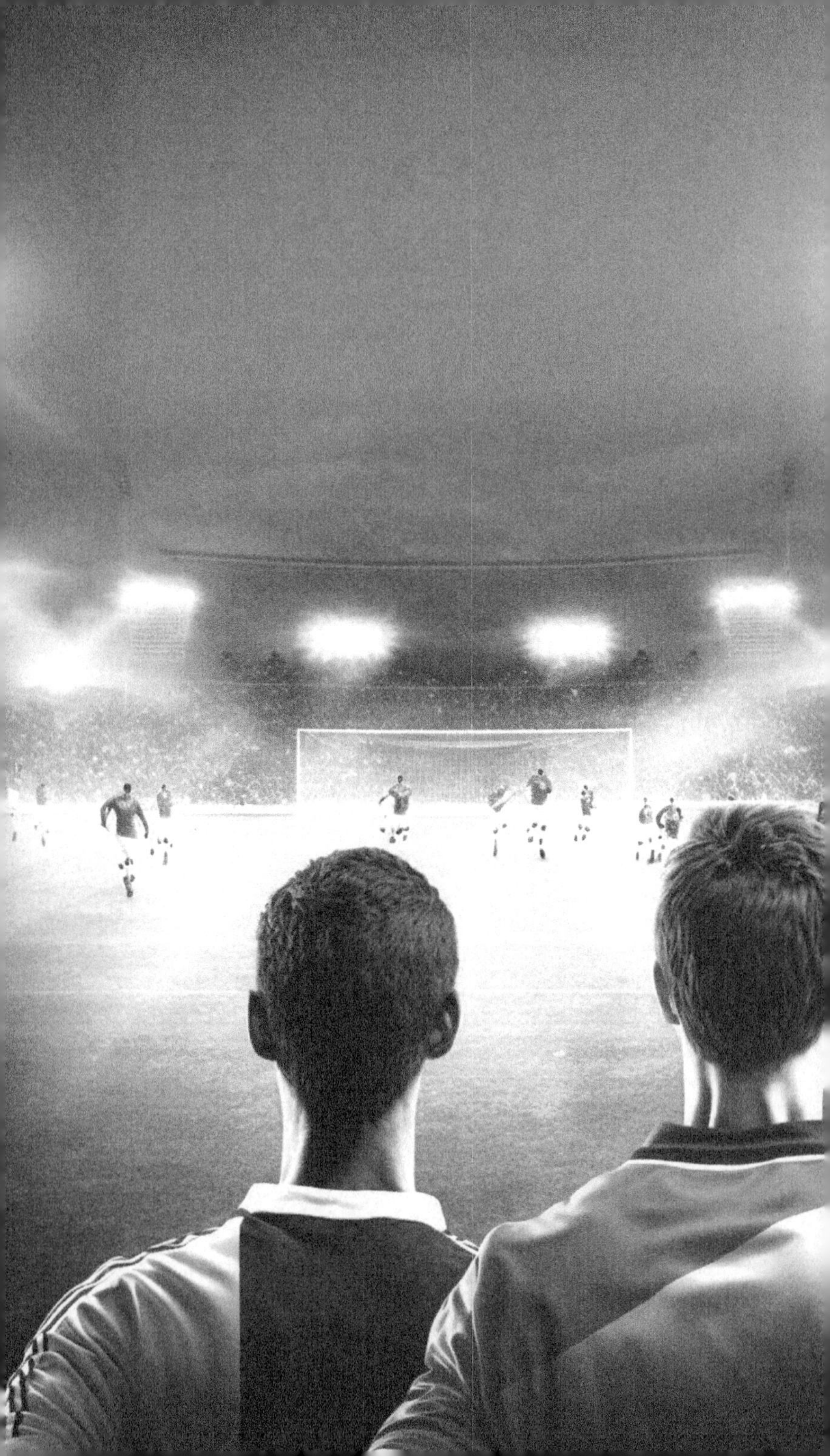

55

Any English football team can aspire to be promoted to the highest league category, the Barclays Premier League.

How is promotion defined?

At the end of each season, the top two teams in the standings, plus the winner of the play-off tournament between teams that finish between third and sixth place, are promoted to the Premier League and are replaced by the three worst teams.

56

During a football match, the distance covered by a player can vary depending on their position on the field and the team's playing style.

Field players usually run more than goalkeepers, and forwards and attacking midfielders tend to have a higher average distance covered than defenders.

On average, it is estimated that a football player covers around 10 kilometers (approximately 6.2 miles) in a match, but this can vary depending on the league, the level of competition, and the team's playing style.

According to some studies, the players who run the most during a match can cover up to 12 kilometers, while those who run the least can cover up to 8 kilometers.

It has also been shown that players run more in the second half of the match than in the first, suggesting that fatigue may be an important factor in the team's performance.

57

In the early days of football, referees used to wear white shirts, but they were often mistaken for players.

As the game became more organized and team uniforms became more standardized, it was decided that referees should have a distinct uniform.

The color black was chosen because it was a neutral color and easily available.

Additionally, black was considered an authoritative color and it was thought that referees would be better respected if they wore it.

On the other hand, goalkeepers began wearing shirts of different colors in 1913 to help referees distinguish them from other players on the field.

The first goalkeeper shirt that was used was bright red in color, and since then goalkeepers have worn a variety of bright colors such as orange, yellow, and green to stand out on the field.

58

The World Cup is one of the most popular sporting events worldwide and attracts a large television audience.

FIFA, the tournament's organizer, has stated that the 2018 edition of the World Cup, held in Russia, had a cumulative global audience of 3.572 billion people, making it the most viewed sporting event in the world.

This figure includes people who followed the tournament on television, online, and mobile devices.

In addition, the World Cup has become an event that transcends the boundaries of sport and has turned into a global celebration that brings people from all over the world together, regardless of their background, culture, or religion.

During the competition, fans gather in public and private places to watch the matches together and cheer on their favorite teams, creating a unique and exciting atmosphere worldwide.

59

Oleg Salenko from Russia holds the record for the most goals scored in a single World Cup match.

He scored 5 goals in Russia's victory over Cameroon.

He looked like a hungry animal every time he appeared near the goal and that's how he demonstrated it.

He achieved five goals, three in the first half and two more in the second half.

"During the match I wasn't thinking about the record. They said something over the loudspeaker, but being focused on the game I didn't hear it very well," expressed the forward, who didn't realize his achievement until some time later.

60

In the Qatar World Cup, the first World Cup to be held in the Middle East is awarded, and it starts in winter to be able to play in a more pleasant climate.

The date change is due to the high temperatures that can reach over 40 degrees Celsius in Qatar in summer.

61

The FIFA World Cup is the most important soccer tournament at the international level and takes place every four years.

Since the first edition in 1930, different countries have hosted the event, and some of them have had the privilege of organizing it more than once.

So far, only five countries have hosted two FIFA World Cups: Mexico, Italy, France, Germany, and Brazil.

-Mexico: The first time this country hosted the World Cup was in 1970, being the first edition held in Latin America. In that year, Brazil was crowned champion. The second time Mexico was the host was in 1986 when Argentina became the champion for the second time in its history.

-Italy: Italy has been the host country in two editions of the FIFA World Cup. The first time was in 1934 when the Italian team became champion for the first time in its history. The second time was in 1990, in an edition where the German team won its third World Cup.

-France: In 1938, France hosted its first World Cup, but failed to advance beyond the quarterfinals. In contrast, in 1998, the French team won its first World Cup as the host country, with an impressive performance from players like Zinedine Zidane.

-Germany: The first time Germany hosted the World Cup was in 1974, and the local team became champion after defeating the Netherlands in the final. The second time was in 2006, when Italy was crowned champion after defeating France in the final.

-Brazil is the country that has won the FIFA World Cup the most times, with a total of five titles. The first time Brazil hosted the event was in 1950, although the final result was one of the biggest surprises in tournament history, as Uruguay won the title at the Maracanã Stadium. The second time Brazil hosted the event was in 2014, and the German team was crowned champion after defeating Argentina in the final.

62

The United States women's national soccer team is one of the most successful in the history of this sport.

Here are some relevant aspects of their trajectory:

-FIFA Women's World Cup: The United States team has won the FIFA Women's World Cup four times, in 1991, 1999, 2015, and 2019. Additionally, they have been runners-up once, in 2011.
The American team has been recognized for their offensive and aggressive style of play, and for featuring some of the most outstanding players in the history of women's soccer, such as Mia Hamm, Abby Wambach, Carli Lloyd, and Megan Rapinoe.

-Olympic Games: The United States women's team has won the gold medal in soccer in four occasions, in 1996, 2004, 2008, and 2012. They have also obtained the silver medal once, in 2000.
In the Tokyo 2021 Olympic Games, the US team won the bronze medal.

-Concacaf Women's Championship: The United States team has won the Concacaf Women's Championship nine times, in 1991, 1993, 1994, 2000, 2002, 2006, 2014, 2018, and 2022.
This tournament is the most important continental competition for women's soccer teams in North America, Central America, and the Caribbean.

-Friendly tournaments: The United States team has also had success in friendly tournaments, such as the Algarve Cup, which they have won ten times, and the SheBelieves Cup, which they have won five times. These tournaments are important for the team's preparation ahead of the most important events, such as the World Cup and the Olympics.

63

Lionel Messi is one of the most recognized and successful football players in the history of the sport.

The following are some relevant aspects of his career:

·**Football trajectory:** Lionel Messi has spent his entire professional career at FC Barcelona, one of the most important clubs in Europe and the world. Since his debut in the first team in 2004, Messi has won countless titles and set several records, both at the club and international level. Among his achievements are 10 Spanish Leagues, 7 Copa del Rey trophies, 4 UEFA Champions Leagues, and 3 FIFA Club World Cups.

·**Individual recognitions:** Messi is one of the most awarded football players in the history of the sport. He has won the Ballon d'Or (the award for the best player in the world) on 7 occasions, more than any other player in history. He has also been chosen as the Best FIFA Men's Player 4 times. In addition, he has been included in the UEFA Team of the Year 11 times and the FIFA FIFPro World11 8 times.

·**Salary and earnings:** Messi has been the highest-paid football player in the world for several years. In his last contract with FC Barcelona, signed in 2017, it was stipulated that he would receive a salary of approximately 40 million euros per year. Additionally, Messi has obtained significant income from sponsorships and advertising. In 2022, he topped the list of the world's highest-paid athletes for the second time, with estimated earnings of $130 million, according to Forbes magazine.

·**Charitable activity:** Messi has also stood out for his charitable and philanthropic work. In 2007, he founded the Leo Messi Foundation, which aims to improve the lives of children and young people in vulnerable situations around the world. Through his foundation, Messi has made donations and carried out projects in different countries.

64

The number 10 on a soccer jersey has become a symbol of quality and talent in the sport, although its origin and meaning vary depending on the region and time period.

In some countries, the number 10 is traditionally assigned to the player who occupies the playmaker or attacking midfielder position, that is, the creative and offensive player responsible for creating goal-scoring opportunities for the team.

In other cases, the number 10 has historically been assigned to standout players or football legends who have worn that number emblematically, such as Pelé, Maradona, Zidane, Ronaldinho, Kaká, and Messi, among others.

Pelé, the legendary Brazilian player, is one of the greatest exponents of the number 10 in the history of soccer.

Pelé wore the number 10 jersey for most of his career and is considered one of the best players of all time.

Diego Maradona, the iconic Argentine player, is also widely associated with the number 10.

Maradona wore that number during his career at Boca Juniors and the Argentine national team, and is remembered for his famous "Hand of God" goal in the 1986 World Cup, as well as his "Goal of the Century" in the same match.

In Colombia, the number 10 has been worn by players such as Carlos Valderrama, known as "El Pibe," who is considered one of the best players in the history of Colombian soccer.

Valderrama was a talented attacking midfielder who played for the Colombian national team and several international clubs.

Currently, the player most associated with the number 10 is Lionel Messi, the Argentine star who has spent most of his career at FC Barcelona.

Messi has worn the number 10 jersey for both the Argentine national team and Barcelona, and is considered one of the greatest football players in history.

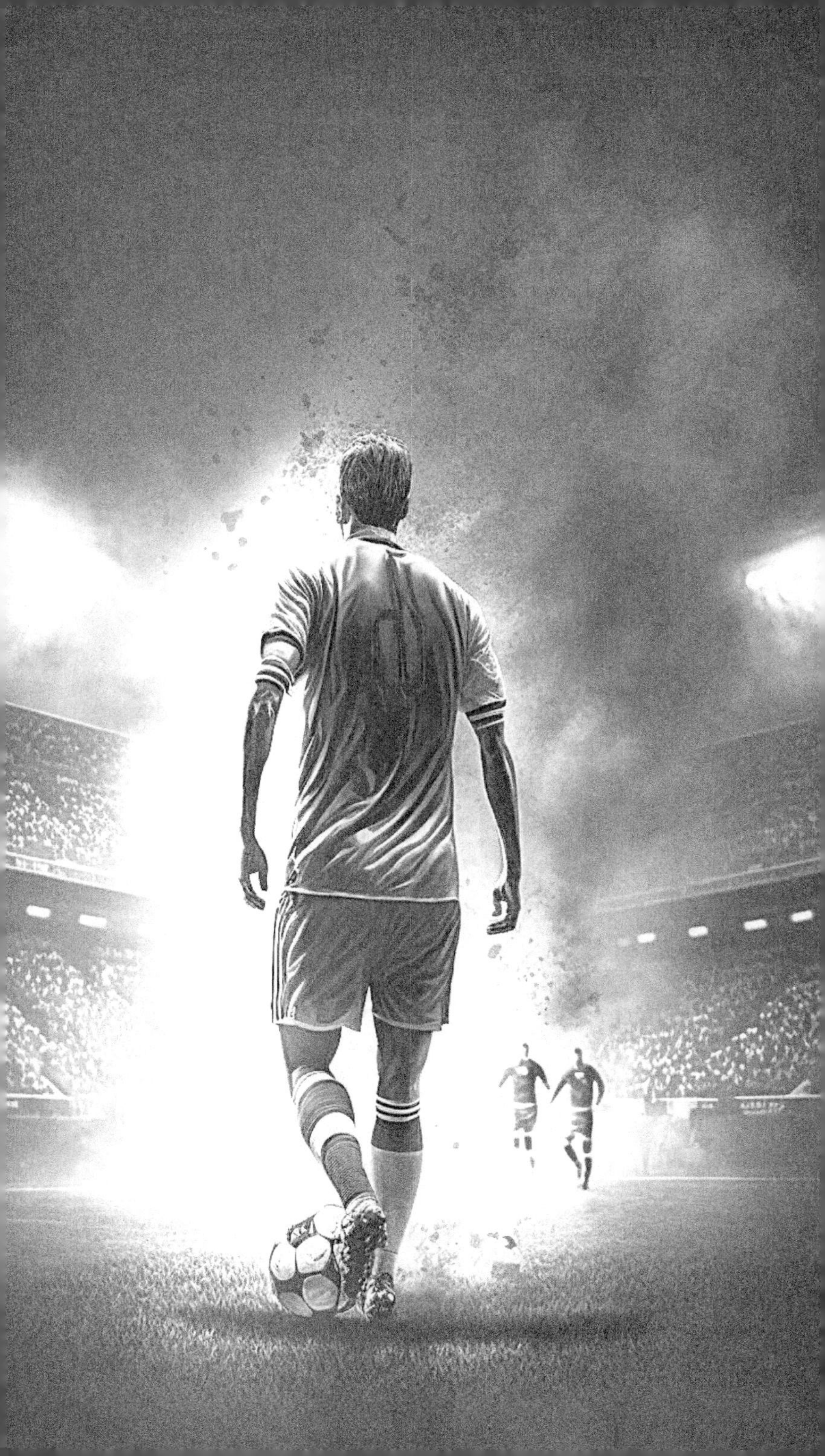

65

The FIFA World Cup, also known as the Football World Cup, is the most coveted trophy in the world's most popular sport.

The trophy, which is awarded to the team that wins the World Cup championship, has evolved over the years.

The first World Cup was held in 1930 in Uruguay, and the original trophy was known as the Jules Rimet Cup.

This trophy was designed by FIFA president Jules Rimet and was made of gilded silver.

It stood at a height of 35 centimeters and weighed 3.8 kilograms.

The trophy depicted Nike, the Greek goddess of victory, holding a football.

The trophy was stolen in 1966 in England but was found by a dog named Pickles.

After Brazil won their third title in 1970, FIFA decided that Brazil could permanently keep the Jules Rimet Cup.

However, in 1983, the Jules Rimet Cup was stolen again and never recovered. In 1974, a new trophy was introduced for the World Cup.

This trophy, known as the FIFA World Cup Trophy, was designed by Italian artist Silvio Gazzaniga and was made of 18-karat gold.

The trophy stands at a height of 36.8 centimeters and weighs 6.1 kilograms. The trophy depicts two human figures holding up the earth.

Before the 1950 World Cup, the Jules Rimet trophy was made of papier-mâché to reduce costs, but this material was not strong enough to withstand the rain.

Therefore, the trophy had to be kept in a special box to protect it from moisture.

After the torrential rain that fell during the 1950 World Cup in Brazil, FIFA decided that it needed a more durable trophy.

66

It is said that Pelé received his nickname because he had six toes on each foot when he was born.

Another version says that, due to his movements as a goalkeeper, he was found to have similarities with the Brazilian goalkeeper Bilé, his father's teammate when he was a player, so they started calling him "Bilé" until the nickname evolved into Pelé.

On the other hand, others claim that the name was given to him because he couldn't pronounce that name properly.

67

Until 1991, football was considered an illegal sport in the state of Mississippi, in the United States.

This law was enacted in 1906 by the state legislature due to the popular belief that football encouraged violence and riots.

As a result, the sport remained largely underground for decades, and only a handful of college and high school teams defied the law and played football in the state.

In 1991, the law was repealed thanks to the efforts of a group of football supporters led by the then-governor of the state, Ray Mabus.

The repeal allowed football to become a legal and popular sport in Mississippi, and today, the state has football teams at all levels, from high school to college and professional football.

68

The Football Association (FA) of England drafted the first official rules of football in 1863, known as "The Laws of the Game."

Before this, football was played informally and each school, college, or community had their own rules.

This meant that it was difficult for teams from different places to play against each other, as the rules varied significantly.

The original rules of football included aspects such as the size of the playing field, the number of players per team, how goals were scored, and how the game was started.

Over the years, these rules have been modified and adjusted to improve player safety and make the game more fair and exciting.

Nowadays, the rules of football are established by the International Federation of Association Football (FIFA) and are used worldwide to ensure uniformity in the practice of the sport.

However, there are still regional variations in some aspects of the game, such as the offside rule, which is interpreted differently in different parts of the world.

69

The spherical shape of a soccer ball is an optical illusion created by its pattern.

If you look closely at a conventional soccer ball, you'll notice that it's not a sphere but a polyhedron that, when inflated with air, takes on a fairly spherical shape.

Specifically, it's a truncated icosahedron; a polyhedron obtained by cutting off the 20 corners of an icosahedron at equal distances from each vertex (one-third of the edge length).

It's composed of 20 regular hexagons and 12 regular pentagons, and has 90 edges.

This polyhedron occupies 86.74% of the volume of its circumscribed sphere; a percentage that increases to 95% when inflated.

70

A 23-year-old Indian footballer died after suffering a serious spinal injury during a goal celebration, in which he attempted a somersault.

Peter Biaksangzuala, of Bethlehem Vengthlang FC, landed on his head while performing a series of flips after scoring the equalizer for his team in a match played in the state of Mizoram, "The Times of India" reported.

Several teammates, unaware of the seriousness of the situation, piled onto him before realizing he was seriously injured.

71

Sir Arthur Conan Doyle, the famous writer and creator of the character Sherlock Holmes, was the first goalkeeper of the Portsmouth Football Club team in England.

Conan Doyle was an avid football fan and in 1882 he joined the Portsmouth Football Club team as a goalkeeper.

At that time, football was still a very incipient sport and the Portsmouth team played in a local league.

Conan Doyle played only a few games with the team before leaving to focus on his writing career, but his brief football career became an interesting curiosity for fans of both football and his literary work.

Throughout his life, Conan Doyle maintained his love for football and in his memoirs he wrote:

"The real thrill in my life as a player came through football."

Despite his brief football career, his contribution to literature is undeniable and his character, Sherlock Holmes, remains one of the most famous and beloved detectives of all time.

72

In youth football leagues, the size of the field is typically adjusted to better suit the ages of the players.

A children's 11-a-side football field should be rectangular, 90 to 120 meters long and 45 to 90 meters wide.

The lines that define it are called touchlines, along the length, and goal lines across the width (1.50 m from the touchline to the fence and from the goal line to the fence).

73

The assertion that Osama Bin Laden, the leader of Al Qaeda, was a big fan of Arsenal and may have attended a match in secret and anonymity has been the subject of speculation for a long time, but it is difficult to determine its veracity.

According to some reports, Bin Laden was a football fanatic and had a particular preference for London's Arsenal.

It has been said that in his propaganda videos, he has often been seen wearing Arsenal jerseys and even had a collection of team match videos.

It has also been speculated that Bin Laden may have attended an Arsenal match at some point in the 1990s.

According to some reports, he may have attended a match at Highbury, Arsenal's former stadium, in complete secrecy and anonymity.

However, there is no concrete evidence to support this claim.

In any case, it is true that football has occasionally been used as a propaganda tool by terrorist and extremist groups.

Some have argued that Bin Laden's love for Arsenal and his use of football in his propaganda videos were part of his strategy to reach out to young people and recruit them to his cause.

74

4 fanbases that are often considered the most passionate.

1. Boca Juniors – Buenos Aires, Argentina: Boca Juniors' fanbase is known as "La 12" and is famous for their passionate support of the team. The fanbase has won numerous awards for their loyalty and creativity, including recognition as "The Best Fanbase in the World" by FIFA.

2. Borussia Dortmund – Dortmund, Germany: Borussia Dortmund's fanbase, known as "Die Gelbe Wand" (The Yellow Wall), is famous for their passion and their ability to create an unforgettable game atmosphere. The fanbase has been praised for their ability to inspire their team even in difficult moments.

3. Liverpool – Liverpool, England: Liverpool's fanbase is known as "The Kop" and is famous for their unconditional support of the team. The fanbase has been present in some of the most iconic moments in football history, including the comeback in the 2005 Champions League final against AC Milan.

4. Celtic – Glasgow, Scotland: Celtic's fanbase is known as "The Bhoys" and is famous for their loyalty and unwavering support of the team. The fanbase has won numerous awards for their passionate support, including recognition as "The Best Fanbase in the World" by FIFA in 2013.

75

Nike is an American sportswear brand known worldwide for its high-quality products, including sports clothing, footwear, and accessories.

Regarding its involvement in the FIFA World Cup, Nike has outfitted several national teams over the years, including Brazil.

In the history of the FIFA World Cup, Brazil has been one of the most successful teams, having won the tournament on five occasions (1958, 1962, 1970, 1994, and 2002).

Nike has been Brazil's equipment supplier in several of these tournaments, including in 2002, when Brazil won its last World Cup.

It is important to note that Nike is not the only sports equipment supplier for national teams in the FIFA World Cup.

Other sports brands such as Adidas, Puma, and Umbro have also outfitted national teams in the tournament.

In summary, Nike has outfitted several national teams in the history of the FIFA World Cup, including Brazil on several occasions.

However, Brazil has only won the tournament once while being outfitted by Nike, and that was in the 2002 edition.

76

Ronaldo Nazario de Lima, also known as "The Phenomenon", is a retired Brazilian football player considered one of the best football players of all time.

He played for several important teams throughout his career, including FC Barcelona and Real Madrid in Spain, and Inter Milan and AC Milan in the Italian Serie A.

Regarding his participation in important derbies, Ronaldo is the only football player in the world who has played in two very prominent derbies in two of the best football leagues in the world.

In Spain, Ronaldo played for both FC Barcelona and Real Madrid, the two most important teams in the country, in the Spanish Clásico.

In Italy, he played for both Inter Milan and AC Milan, the two biggest teams in Milan, in the Milan derby.

Throughout his career, Ronaldo won many titles and achievements, including two World Cups with the Brazilian national team in 1994 and 2002.

He also won the UEFA Golden Boot as the top scorer in Europe twice, in 1997 and 2002.

In addition, he won the FIFA Ballon d'Or three times, in 1997, 2002, and 2003.

77

Brazil is a world-renowned soccer team and one of the most successful in the history of the sport.

Since the first FIFA World Cup was founded in 1930, Brazil has participated in every tournament, meaning they have been present in all 21 World Cup championships held to date, including the latest one in Russia in 2018.

The Brazilian national team has been one of the most dominant in the history of soccer, winning a total of five World Cups, making them the second most successful team in the tournament's history, second only to the Argentina national soccer team.

Brazil has also been a finalist on two other occasions and has reached the semi-finals on five other occasions.

In terms of geography, the World Cup has been played on four different continents, with Europe and the Americas hosting the most tournaments.

Eleven of the 21 World Cups have been played in Europe, while eight have been held in the Americas.

In addition, one tournament has been played in Asia and another in Africa.

78

Fernando das Neves was a Portuguese footballer who played as a defender for several clubs in Portugal, including Sporting de Braga and Benfica.

However, what he is most remembered for is his tragic death during a football match.

On November 13, 1973, das Neves was playing a league match between his hometown team, S.C. Olhanense, and Uniao de Tomar.

The match was in the 13th minute when das Neves collapsed on the field due to a heart attack.

Efforts to save das Neves' life were in vain and the footballer passed away on the field.

The news of his death shocked the football community and was one of the first documented cases of a player dying during a football match.

Following the tragedy, measures were taken to improve the health and safety conditions for footballers, including increased medical supervision and better first aid training for staff at stadiums.

79

Sócrates Brasileiro Sampaio de Souza Vieira de Oliveira, better known as Sócrates, was a Brazilian footballer who excelled both on and off the field.

In addition to being an exceptional player, Sócrates was a political activist and advocate for democracy in Brazil.

The former Brazilian player Sócrates said in 1983: "I want to die on a Sunday and with Corinthians as champions."

Sócrates continued to play football for several years after making this statement, but eventually retired from professional sport in 1989.

He died on a Sunday in 2011, one hour after Corinthians became Brazilian champions.

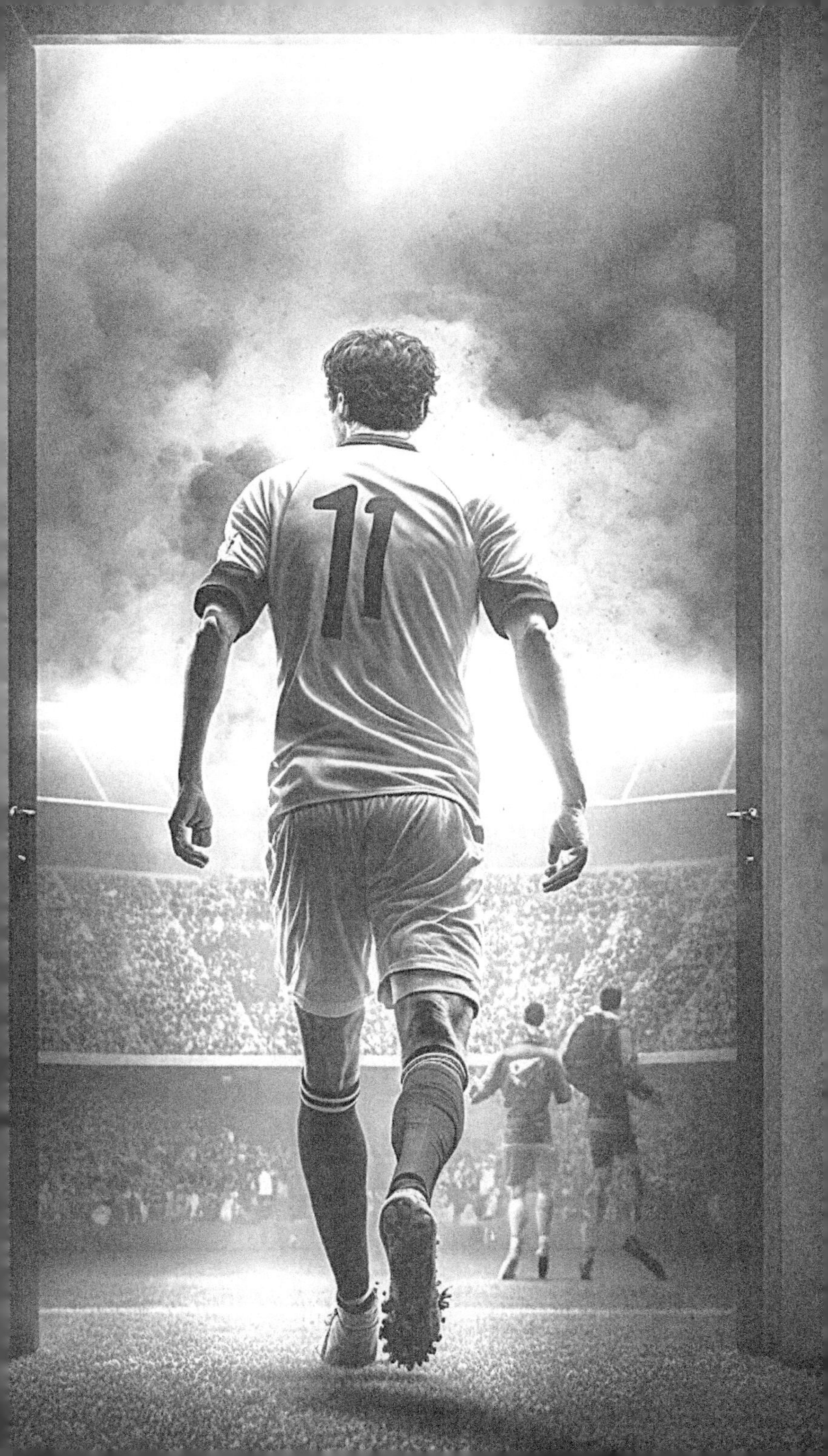
11

80

Diego Armando Maradona is considered one of the best football players in history, but it's true that he never played a Copa Libertadores match, the most important club competition in South America.

The main reason why Maradona never participated in the Copa Libertadores is because during the time he played in Argentina, only the two champions of the national tournaments (Torneo Metropolitano and Torneo Nacional) qualified for the continental competition.

Maradona began his career at Argentinos Juniors in 1976, and at that time, the team had not won any national titles, so they couldn't qualify for the Copa Libertadores.

In 1981, Maradona joined Boca Juniors, which had won several titles, but again, only the champions of the Torneo Metropolitano and Torneo Nacional had the right to participate in the Copa Libertadores.

During his career, Maradona won several titles with Boca Juniors and other teams such as Barcelona, Napoli, and the Argentine national team, but he never had the chance to play in the Copa Libertadores.

It is important to note that the situation has since changed, and currently, Argentine teams have several opportunities to qualify for the Copa Libertadores through different national and regional competitions.

81

The New York Cosmos is a professional soccer team founded in 1970 that played in the North American Soccer League (NASL) and was one of the most successful teams of its time.

During its existence, the club had a very particular mascot: a chimpanzee named Harold.

Harold was adopted by the New York Cosmos in the 1970s and became a popular attraction among fans of the team.

He was often seen dressed in the team's jersey and cheering from the stands. It is also said that on some occasions he participated in the halftime show, performing tricks for the entertainment of the spectators.

However, in 1980, during a game at Giants Stadium in New Jersey, Harold bit Cosmos player Franz Beckenbauer on the leg.

The incident caused the animal to be banned from the team's games and its permission to attend any sporting events was revoked.

It was said that Harold had been provoked by some fans who were throwing food and drink at him, which had made him nervous and aggressive.

After the incident, Harold was taken to a primate sanctuary in Maryland where he spent the rest of his life.

The episode served as a wake-up call about the risks of having wild animals as pets, and led to sports authorities banning the presence of animals in stadiums.

82

The first set of rules for modern football was created in 1863 by the Football Association (FA) in England.

In that original set of rules, there was no goalkeeper position. Instead, field players would rotate to defend the goal when needed.

The goalkeeper position was incorporated into football eight years later in 1871 when it was allowed for a player to stay in the goal to defend it.

As for the goals, it was specified that they should be defined by two vertical posts separated by a distance of eight yards (approximately 7.32 meters) and there should be no tape or bar between them.

This measure is still in place in professional football today.

In addition, the team that won the initial coin toss could choose which goal to defend and the losing team had to kick off from the center of the field.

This rule is also still in place today.

It should be noted that over the years, numerous modifications have been made to the original rules, but these aspects remain fundamental in the game of football.

83

Pele is widely recognized as one of the greatest football players of all time and is credited with the record for being the top scorer in professional football with a total of 1,259 goals in 1,363 matches.

However, there is some controversy surrounding this number and some argue that the actual number of goals may be different.

Part of the controversy is due to the fact that data from some of the competitions in which Pelé participated is not fully documented, especially friendly matches and some regional tournaments in Brazil.

Additionally, some of the matches in which goals are attributed to Pelé have not been properly verified, which has led some experts to question the accuracy of the 1,259 goal figure.

Another factor to consider is that Pelé's record includes goals scored in non-official matches, i.e., friendly and exhibition matches.

If only goals scored in official matches, such as national leagues, national and international cups, and international matches are considered, then Pelé's record is reduced to 767 goals in 831 matches.

Despite these controversies, it is widely accepted that Pelé is one of the most talented and successful players in the history of football, and his goal-scoring record remains impressive regardless of the exact number.

84

The longest football match in history was played in 2017 in the Brazilian city of Jataí.

The match was organized for charitable purposes to raise funds for the local hospital and lasted a total of 36 hours, surpassing the previous record of 35 hours and 30 minutes.

The match was played by two teams of 11 players each and was played on a full-sized football field.

The players were in action the entire time, with no breaks, and could only change players after being on the field for at least an hour.

The final result of the match was 333 goals for and 293 against, with the team scoring the most goals winning.

The event organizers said that the match was a great success and that they were able to raise a significant amount of money for the local hospital.

It is important to note that, despite being a record in terms of duration, this match is not considered an official football match as it was not played according to the rules of any official league or competition.

Additionally, these types of charity matches often have more flexible rules and a more playful approach, which can allow for many goals to be scored.

85

The football team with the longest name is a team called Llanfairpwllgwyngyllgogerychwyrndrobwlllantysiliogogogo.

It is the longest place name in the United Kingdom and the third longest in the world.

The team is located on the island of Anglesey in Wales, and its name corresponds to the village it represents.

86

Officially, the first time a football match was broadcast on television for the whole of Spain was on February 15th, 1959, in a classic match between Real Madrid and Barcelona, played at Chamartín.

In the Catalan capital, the supply of black and white televisions in stores was exhausted.

According to the chronicles of the moment, electronic stores on the Ramblas in Barcelona opened on Sunday to tune in the match on their televisions.

Hundreds of people crowded in front of the shop windows, with children sitting on shoulders, to follow the match from a distance.

At that time, there were barely 10,000 televisions in Spain.

⚽

87

In Italy 1934, Egypt made history by becoming the first African country to participate in a FIFA World Cup.

Egypt entered the competition as the African champions after winning the Africa Cup of Nations in 1957.

However, Egypt came very close to participating in the first edition of the World Cup, which was held in Uruguay in 1930.

FIFA had invited several teams from different parts of the world to participate in the tournament, and Egypt was one of them.

Egypt accepted the invitation, but the voyage by boat from Africa to South America was long and expensive, so they could not arrive in time for the start date of the tournament.

Eventually, the Egyptian national team could not participate in the 1930 World Cup, but their presence was a huge step forward for football in Africa and laid the foundation for future participations of African teams in the World Cup.

Since then, several African teams have participated in the World Cup, including Morocco, Tunisia, Algeria, Nigeria, Cameroon, Senegal, Ghana, Ivory Coast, and South Africa, among others.

Today, African football is constantly growing and has proven to be a highly competitive region in international football.

88

The Football World Cup resumed after World War II with the Brazil 1950 edition.

Due to their roles during the war, Japan and Germany were banned from the competition.

Italy, however, was allowed to participate in the 1950 World Cup, despite its involvement in the conflict.

This was largely due to the intervention of Ottorino Barassi, who protected the World Cup from being stolen by Nazi forces during World War II.

Barassi was the Secretary General of the Italian Football Federation and was in charge of the trophy's custody at the time of the war.

Barassi, in an act of bravery and patriotism, decided to hide the World Cup in a shoebox under his bed to prevent it from being stolen by the Nazis.

After the war, FIFA thanked Barassi for his bravery by allowing Italy to participate in the 1950 World Cup, even though the country had been part of the Axis during World War II.

In the 1950 World Cup, Italy did not perform well and was eliminated in the group stage, however, their participation was a symbol of reconciliation and a step forward in the reconstruction of the world after the war.

89

The biggest victory in the history of the FIFA World Cup occurred during the 1982 edition in Spain, in a group stage match between Hungary and El Salvador.

The game was played in the city of Elche on June 15th, 1982. Hungary, who had world-class players such as Sandor Kocsis, Ferenc Puskas, and Zoltan Czibor, showed their superiority from the beginning of the match and scored the first goal at 10 minutes.

El Salvador, who was a much weaker team, couldn't resist the Hungarian dominance and quickly found themselves behind on the scoreboard.

By the end of the first half, Hungary was already winning 3-0, and in the second half, the difference in quality and skill became even more evident.

Hungary scored seven more goals, including a hat-trick from Sandor Kocsis, to end the match with an impressive 10-1 victory.

This win was the biggest victory in the history of the FIFA World Cup and is still remembered as one of the most dominant performances in the tournament's history.

Meanwhile, El Salvador failed to qualify for the next round and finished last in their group.

90

The fastest goal in the history of the FIFA World Cup occurred in the third place play-off of the 2002 edition, played between South Korea and Turkey.

The match took place in the city of Daegu, South Korea on June 29, 2002.

Just 11 seconds after the initial whistle, Turkish forward Hakan Sukur scored the fastest goal in World Cup history.

The goal resulted from a quick attacking play by Turkey, which caught the South Korean defense off guard.

After recovering the ball in midfield, Turkish midfielder Emre Belözoğlu sent a long pass to Hakan Sukur, who controlled the ball with his chest and shot it towards the opponent's goal to score the historic goal.

Hakan Sukur's goal was not only the fastest in World Cup history, but it was also the first in Turkey's 3-2 victory over South Korea in that third place play-off.

Hakan Sukur, who played for Galatasaray in Turkey and Inter Milan in Italy during his football career, is considered one of the best forwards in the history of Turkish football, and his fastest goal in the World Cup is remembered as one of the most exciting moments in the history of the tournament.

91

The first own goal in the history of the FIFA World Cup was scored by Brazilian defender Marcelo during the opening match of the 2014 edition in Brazil.

The match was played on June 12, 2014, at the Arena de Sao Paulo stadium and pitted Brazil against Croatia.

In the 11th minute of the match, Marcelo tried to intercept a Croatian striker's cross but unfortunately ended up deflecting the ball into his own goal, giving Croatia an early lead in the game.

Despite this initial setback, Brazil managed to come back and eventually won the match 3-1.

Four years later, in the final of the 2018 FIFA World Cup, Croatian forward Mario Mandzukic scored the second own goal in World Cup history during the match against France.

The goal came in the 18th minute of the game, when French defender Antoine Griezmann sent a free kick into the Croatian area and Mandzukic, in his attempt to clear the ball, ended up deflecting it into his own goal.

Despite this setback, Croatia fought to recover but eventually lost the match 4-2 to France.

Mandzukic's own goal was the first in a FIFA World Cup final and one of the most unfortunate moments in World Cup history.

92

The use of cards in football was first introduced during the 1970 FIFA World Cup, which was held in Mexico.

The person responsible for its introduction was the British referee Ken Aston. In a quarterfinal match between England and Argentina, played on June 7, 1970, Aston found himself in a situation where he needed to make a disciplinary decision.

After a serious foul, the Argentine players surrounded the referee demanding a red card for the English player who committed the foul.

Aston felt confused and frustrated by the lack of a clear system for sanctioning players, and while driving back to his hotel after the match, he came up with the idea of using yellow and red cards to indicate fouls.

The card system, according to Aston, was simple and easy to understand for players, referees, and spectators.

Yellow cards would be used to caution a player and red cards to send them off. Aston presented his proposal to FIFA, which accepted it and incorporated it into its official rules of play in 1971.

Since then, the card system has been adopted worldwide and has become an integral part of football.

93

The first penalty save in World Cup history occurred during the Round of 16 match between Brazil and Spain at the 1934 FIFA World Cup held in Italy.

The match was played on May 27, 1934 at the San Siro stadium in Milan.

20 minutes into the game, the Belgian referee Louis Baert awarded a penalty to Spain for a foul committed by Brazilian defender Machado inside the box.

The penalty taker was Spanish forward Isidro Lángara, who shot with power and direction towards the center of the Brazilian goal.

However, Brazilian goalkeeper Jaguaré managed to save the shot and prevent the Spanish goal.

This was the first penalty save in World Cup history, and a historic moment for the Brazilian goalkeeper and his team.

Despite the penalty save, Brazil eventually lost the match 3-1 to Spain, who advanced to the quarter-finals of the tournament.

94

The match between Portugal and the Netherlands in the Round of 16 of the 2006 World Cup in Germany is remembered as one of the most violent matches in World Cup history.

During the match, a total of 16 yellow cards and 4 red cards were issued, setting a new record for the number of expulsions and cards in a single World Cup match.

The match was played on June 25, 2006, at the Nuremberg Stadium, and from the beginning, it was played intensively and aggressively.

Players from both teams committed numerous fouls, and there were several confrontations between them.

The Russian referee Valentin Ivanov was forced to show numerous yellow cards and send off four players, two from each team.

The players who were sent off were Portuguese Costinha, Dutch Khalid Boulahrouz, Portuguese Deco, and Dutch Giovanni van Bronckhorst.

The aggressiveness of the match and the record number of yellow and red cards caused a great deal of controversy and criticism from the media and fans.

However, the match had a significant impact on the history of the World Cup and is remembered as one of the most violent and controversial matches in the competition.

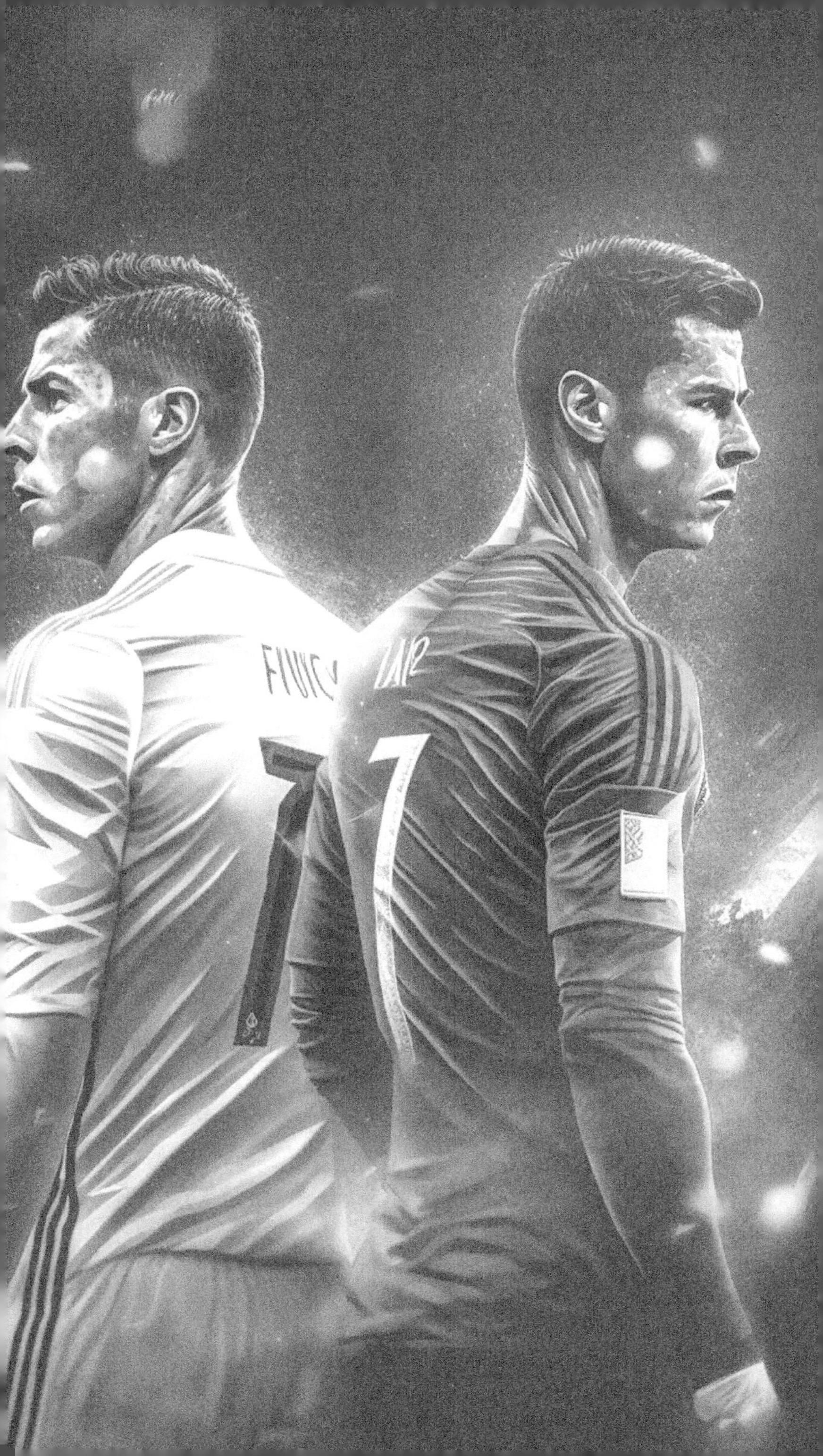

95

Bernd Trautmann is a retired German football goalkeeper who arrived in England as a paratrooper of the German Luftwaffe during World War II.

Trautmann was born on October 22, 1923 in Bremen, Germany, and joined the Luftwaffe in 1941 at the age of 17.

In 1945, at the age of 21, he was captured by British troops while fighting on the Western front and was sent to a prisoner of war camp in Cheshire, England.

There he started playing football with other prisoners of war and caught the attention of local clubs with his skills as a goalkeeper.

In 1948, after being released from captivity, Trautmann joined the amateur team St Helens Town and later Manchester City in the English First Division.

During his career, Trautmann became one of the most prominent goalkeepers in the history of English football, being considered by many as one of the best of his era.

In his career with Manchester City, Trautmann played over 500 games and won the FA Cup in 1956, in a match that is remembered for his heroic performance despite suffering a broken neck during the game.

He also played for the Everton team before retiring in 1964.

Despite his German origins and past as a member of the Luftwaffe, Trautmann was highly respected in England for his ability on the field and dedication to football.

In 2004, he was appointed Officer of the Order of the British Empire by Queen Elizabeth II in recognition of his service to football and his work in promoting friendship between Germany and the United Kingdom.

96

**Diego Forlán won the Copa América 2011
just like his father Pablo did in 1967
and his maternal grandfather,
Juan Carlos in 1959 and 1967.**

Papa Pablo, a left-back, played for Peñarol,
Sao Paulo, Cruzeiro, Nacional,
and Defensor Sporting.

He won the Copa América in 1967 with his
father-in-law Corazzo as the coach.

Grandfather Juan Carlos Corazzo, a midfielder,
won a gold medal at the 1928 Olympics and
the 1930 World Cup with the
Uruguayan national team.

He was called "the Kid", was a coach, and won
two Copa América titles in 1959 and 1967.

97

The penalty kick, or simply penalty, was introduced in football around 1891 as a way to punish fouls committed inside the penalty area that would have likely prevented a goal.

Before the introduction of the penalty kick, fouls inside the area would often result in a free kick, but this was not always sufficient to adequately punish offenders.

In the early penalty rules, the goalkeeper was allowed to move up to 5 meters forward before the kick was taken.

This was done to increase the defending team's chances of stopping the penalty kick and making the result more uncertain.

However, this rule was modified over time, and today, goalkeepers must remain on their goal line until the kick is taken.

The introduction of the penalty kick was an important milestone in the history of football, as it allowed for proper punishment of offenders inside the area and increased the likelihood of goals being scored.

Although there have been some changes to the rules over time, the penalty kick remains a fundamental part of modern football and a source of excitement and drama for fans around the world.

98

The claim that Italian player Giuseppe Meazza's pants fell down during a penalty in the 1938 World Cup semifinal is not true.

In fact, Giuseppe Meazza, who was one of the most famous and important players in Italian football, did not participate in the 1938 World Cup due to an injury.

It was the Brazilian player Leônidas da Silva who played in that semifinal against Italy, which Brazil ultimately won 2-1.

It's possible that the story of pants falling down during a penalty originated from some other football match or event, but it's not related to the 1938 World Cup semifinal between Italy and Brazil.

False stories are often spread on the internet, and it's important to verify the accuracy of information before sharing or believing it.

99

On September 21, 1986, in a First Division match between West Ham United and Newcastle United, West Ham United won the game by a hefty score of 8-1, with Alvin Martin scoring a rather unique hat-trick.

During the match, West Ham United defender Alvin Martin scored three goals against three different goalkeepers of Newcastle United.

The first goal came against the starting goalkeeper, Martin Thomas, in the 10th minute. Then, in the 47th minute, he scored the second goal against Chris Hedworth, who had replaced Thomas after an injury.

Finally, in the 60th minute, he scored the third goal against Peter Beardsley, who had taken the gloves after Hedworth was sent off for committing a last-man foul.

This unique achievement by Alvin Martin still stands as a record in the English football league, and has become a memorable moment in the history of West Ham United.

The final score of 8-1 is also one of the widest victories in the history of the English Premier League.

100

Modern football originated in Britain in the second half of the 19th century and, in its early years, it was a violent and chaotic sport with few clear rules.

Richard Mulcaster (1531-1611) was an English educator, known for promoting sport and physical exercise in schools, including football.

Mulcaster is not recognized as the sole responsible for the elimination of violence in football, but he is credited with establishing some of the earliest rules and principles that helped shape modern football.

In his work "Positions", written in 1581, Mulcaster proposed basic rules for the game of football that included the prohibition of grabbing or hitting players, and the use of a round ball.

Additionally, Mulcaster emphasized the importance of fair play and respect towards the opponent.

Over time, other important figures in football, such as Ebenezer Cobb Morley, pushed for clearer and unified rules that gave rise to modern football.

However, Mulcaster's influence in promoting a fairer and less violent game in early football is recognized by many historians and sports enthusiasts.

101

The use of numbers on football players' shirts was first regulated at the 1954 World Cup in Switzerland.

Until then, players did not have fixed numbers on their shirts, and referees had to identify them by name or physical characteristics.

At this World Cup, it was decided that each player should wear a number on the back of their shirt, and that number should remain the same throughout the tournament.

This facilitated the identification of players by referees, journalists, and spectators.

Regarding the absence of the Argentine national team in the 1950 and 1954 World Cups, it was mainly due to economic and political problems affecting the country at that time.

In 1958, the Argentine team returned to participate in a World Cup in Sweden, and that was the first tournament in which Argentine players wore fixed numbers on their shirts.

Since then, the use of numbers on football players' shirts has become a common practice in football and has become a way to identify players and their positions on the field.

If you have enjoyed the football curiosities presented in this book, we would like to ask you to share a review on Amazon.

Your opinion is very valuable to us and to other football enthusiasts who are looking to be entertained and learn new knowledge about this sport.

We understand that leaving a comment can be a tedious process, but we ask that you take a few minutes of your time to share your thoughts and opinions with us.

Your support is very important to us and helps us to continue creating quality content for lovers of this amazing sport.

We appreciate your support and hope that you have enjoyed reading our book as much as we enjoyed writing it.

Thank you for sharing your experience with us!

★ ★ ★ ★ ★

Printed in Great Britain
by Amazon